Pass the Life in the UK Test Practice Questions and Answers

As part of this product you have also received FREE access to online tests that will help you to pass the Life in the UK Test Practice Questions and Answers
To gain access, simply go to:

www.MyLifeInTheUKTest.net

Orders:

You can order through Amazon.co.uk under ISBN: 978-1-911259-077, or through Gardners.com.

ISBN: 978-1-911259-077

First published in 2016.

Disclaimer

Every effort has been made to ensure that the information contained within this guide is accurate at the time of publication. The publisher is not responsible for anyone failing any part of any selection process as a result of the information contained within this guide. The publisher and their authors cannot accept any responsibility for any errors or omissions within this guide, however caused. No responsibility for loss or damage occasioned by any person acting, or refraining from action, as a result of the material in this publication can be accepted by the publisher.

The information within this guide does not represent the views of any third party service or organisation.

Contents

INTRODUCTION

Hello, and welcome to your guide, *Life in the UK Test: Practice Questions and Answers.* If you are reading this, then the chances are you've decided to become a British citizen. This is a brave and exciting choice which will have fantastic benefits for you. However, it's also time consuming and expensive. The application process is long and arduous.

Luckily, this guide is here to help!

The second book in our *British Citizen Series*, this guide will provide you with 21 full mock tests. Every single one of our tests is laid out exactly like the real thing, meaning that this book is the PERFECT resource to help you practise for your assessment!

Our advice is to use this book in conjunction with the first book in our series, *Life in the UK Test: Study Guide.* The materials from the aforementioned book have been taken from the Home Office Publication, *Life in the United Kingdom: a guide for new residents.* This means that everything we've tested you on in this guide and our previous guide; is based on what you can be expected to encounter during the real thing.

The material from this book will test you on the knowledge needed for the **third edition** of the test, which was launched in 2013.

At the time of writing (November 2016) the price to take the Life in the UK Test is a whopping £50. Every time you re-take, you'll need to pay out beforehand. Thus you won't just be spending your time, but your money too! Hopefully this should give you even more incentive to pass the first time!

The aim of this book is to help you SAVE money. By using this guide, and our companion books, you can make sure that you ace your first attempt at the test. With our help, and the right commitment, you truly can become a certified British citizen.

How to Use This Guide

To pass the Life in the UK Test, you'll need to revise extremely hard. There are an awful lot of topics that you'll need to revise, from history to politics. To help make the learning process as easy as possible, we've replicated the real tests as closely as possible. Each test in this book contains a wide mixture of questions, with all of the tests focusing on topics such as British history, modern day Britain and politics.

At the back of the book, you'll find all of the answers to the questions, so you can check up on how well you are doing. You can take the tests in any order that you like, but we recommend spending a maximum of 45 minutes on each test; to reflect the real thing.

Before we begin, let's go over what you need to do in order to become a resident of the UK.

Applying to Become a Resident of the UK

In order to become a citizen of the United Kingdom, you'll need the following:

- You must be able to speak and read in English;

- You must have a good understanding of living in the UK, and what this requires;

- You must be able to pass the Life in the UK Test.

In order to become a British citizen, you will need to provide good evidence that you have speaking and listening skills in English at B1 level of the European Framework of Reference. There are a wide variety of tests that you can take and these tests vary in whether they test speaking and listening skills only, or combine this with reading and writing tests.

In this book, we'll provide you with essential knowledge that will help you prepare for taking the Life in the UK Test.

The Life in the UK Test

The Life in the UK Test is a computer-based assessment. Passing the test is one of the requirements for anyone who is seeking Indefinite Leave to Remain in the United Kingdom, or seeking naturalisation as a British citizen. You won't need to take the test if you are under the age of 18, or over the age of 65. Once you have passed, you won't need to take the test again.

The test will assess you on your knowledge of Britain's past and present. While you won't need to remember dates of birth or death, you will need to have a strong historical understanding of Britain in order to pass.

The Life in the UK Test has 24 multiple-choice questions, and lasts for 45 minutes. The questions are chosen at random, and in order to pass, you need to achieve a mark of at least 75%. So that means, out of 24 questions, you will need to get at least 18 correct. The test is taken in English, although special arrangements can be made for anyone who would prefer to take the test in Welsh or in Scottish Gaelic.

In order to take the Life in the UK Test, you'll need to book your test online at https://www.gov.uk/life-in-the-uk-test. The test can only be taken at a government registered test centre. There are 60 Life in the UK Test centres across the UK. If you take the test at any other establishment, without governmental permission, the results will be not be accepted.

When you book your test, you will need:

- **An email address.** This will be used to contact you/confirm your test date;

- **A debit or credit card.** To take payment for the test;

- **An accepted form of ID.** To ensure that you are a legitimate candidate. Accepted forms of ID include: a passport (which can be out of date), a UK driving licence, an EU identity card, an immigration status document with a UK residence permit, or a biometric residence permit.

When booking your test, it is essential that the name given on your test booking matches exactly with the ID that you use to book the test. You must include your full name, with any middle names, or you will be rejected.

After you've booked your test, you may need to wait for a short while before taking it. You are able to cancel your test without charge for up to 7 days after booking, but after those 7 days, you will not receive a refund in the event of cancellation.

Once you arrive at the test centre, you'll need to be registered, so make sure you get there as early as possible. You'll be required to sign a document confirming your attendance, and will be given the opportunity to undergo some practice questions prior to taking the actual test. These questions won't count towards your actual mark, and are just there to help you become familiar with the testing software.

If you pass the test, then you will be provided with a Pass Notification Letter. You'll need to sign this before you leave the centre, before taking it with you and sending it off as part of your citizenship application. It is essential that you keep this safe, as you won't be able to get a replacement.

In the event that you fail, you'll be eligible to book and pay for the test again, but you'll need to wait for at least 7 days before doing so.

Why Do I Need to Take the Test?

The Life in the UK Test provides demonstrable proof that you have sufficient knowledge of life and language in the United Kingdom. If you are applying for Indefinite Leave to Remain (also known as 'Settlement') or British citizenship, then you'll need to take this.

In order to meet the requirements, you'll need to:

- Pass the Life in the UK Test;

- Obtain a speaking and listening qualification in English at B1 CEFR or higher, or its equivalent. If you have a degree-level qualification or higher, in English, then you won't need to take a language test. Likewise, you won't need to take a language test if you are from a country where English is the majority spoken language.

Which Areas Should I Study?

As mentioned, you should try to learn as much as you possibly can from the chapters of our previous book. All of the material is testable and could appear in your exam. However, you will not need to remember dates of birth or death. Instead, you will be expected to know when key events happened, or when particular individuals lived. For example, you won't be asked 'What year was Shakespeare born in?' but you might be asked, 'In 1564, which famous playwright was born?'

In regards to learning dates, there are also a few exceptions. You will need to know the dates for important festivals and events. For example, if you are asked what date Christmas falls on, you will be expected to answer with December 25th. Likewise, with movable festivals such as Easter, you'll need to know the month of the year in which they occur.

When it comes to learning about famous figures, events and even law, you'll need to take a very comprehensive approach. By this we mean that you need to learn everything in the text, not just one or two things. For example, you can't just learn that Charlie Chaplin was an actor. You need to learn that he was an actor in silent movies, who became one of the first British talents to make it into Hollywood. Learn all of the facts collectively, and then be able to explain them in your own way.

Now that we've looked at the test, let's begin your practice papers.

Good luck!

TEST 1

Q1. Members of the Northern Ireland Assembly meet in Belfast. True or false?

A – True

B – False

Q2. If you are unable to vote in person, then you can submit your vote via:

A – Text message

B – Carrier pigeon

C – Email

D – Post

Q3. The role of the Home Secretary is to:

A – Manage the country's economy

B – Manage the country's security services

C – Manage the country's birth control

D – Manage the country's medical services

Q4. During the Bronze Age, people lived in what became known as 'bronze houses'. True or false?

A – True

B – False

Q5. St Augustine was rewarded for his missionary efforts, by being made Archbishop of Canterbury. True or false?

A – True

B – False

Q6. Which of the following statements is true?

A – One of the negative sides to the Industrial Revolution was the poor working conditions, where there were very few laws in place to protect employees.

B – One of the positive sides to the Industrial Revolution was the improvement of working conditions, with new laws being introduced to protect employees.

Q7. How many people sit on a jury in England?

A – 9

B – 16

C – 6

D – 12

Q8. Once you reach the age of 70, you will need to renew your driving licence every:

A – 2 years

B – 9 years

C – 3 years

D – 5 years

Q9. During the Civil War, the supporters of King Charles I were known as 'the Roundheads'. True or false?

A – True

B – False

Q10. Who was the author of *The Jungle Book*?

A – Roald Dahl

B – Rudyard Kipling

C – Enid Blyton

D – Salman Rushdie

Q11. Why does the Welsh dragon not appear on the Union Flag?

A – Wales is not yet considered a valid part of Britain.

B – The dragon is aesthetically unpleasing.

C – Wales was already united with England when the Union Flag was created.

D – As the creators of the flag, Wales saw no reason for their sign to be on it.

Q12. Sir William Walton was the composer of which of the following:

A – *Annie and the Five Lambs*

B – *Shavosky's Fifth*

C – *Ode to Thy Wicked Earl*

D – *Belshazzar's Feast*

Q13. Which two of the following are plays written by William Shakespeare:

A – *Romeo and Juliet*

B – *The Duchess of Malfi*

C – *The Taming of the Shrew*

D – *Star Wars*

Q14. In 1348, which of the following diseases arrived in England?

A – Ebola

B – The Black Death

C – The Millennium Bug

D – Herpes

Q15. Who deals with complaints about the police in Scotland?

A – The Chief of Police Recruitment

B – The Police Complaints Commissioner

C – The Police Complaints and Pensions Department

D – Any local police officer

Q16. Which of the below statements is true?

A – The National Citizen Service provides 16-17 year olds with the chance to develop their skills and take part in community schemes.

B – The National Citizen Service provides 16-17 year old offenders with the chance to rehabilitate themselves and become upstanding members of society.

Q17. Which two of the following are security services operating in the UK, to prevent crime and terrorism?

A – NI5

B – MI5

C – GCHU

D – GCHQ

Q18. Which national flower is commonly associated with Scotland?

A – The Shamrock

B – The Dandelion

C – The Thistle

D – The Rose

Q19. The Falklands Islands are a part of the UK. True or false?

A – True

B – False

Q20. During your citizenship ceremony, you will have to recite which of the following:

A – The pledge of sovereignty

B – The oath of allegiance

C – The oath of fealty

D – The pledge of honourability

Q21. Damien Hirst and Richard Wright are both winners of which prestigious award?

A – The Turner Prize

B – The Mercury Music Prize

C – A BAFTA award

D – The Laurence Olivier award

Q22. You can be ruled out of participating in jury duty, if:

A – You are busy at work

B – You have an important lunch to attend

C – It falls during your holiday from work

D – You have certain criminal convictions

Q23. Which of the following statements is true?

A – Boxing Day is a public holiday in the UK

B – Boxing Day is not a public holiday in the UK

Q24. What did the suffragettes campaign for?

A – The right for women to vote

B – The right for working class votes

C – Free medical treatment

D – A female prime minister

TEST 2

Q1. Which of the following poets wrote *She Walks In Beauty*?

A – Robert Browning

B – Katie Noakes

C – Lord Byron

D – William Blake

Q2. Elizabeth I was the daughter of:

A – James II and his wife Margaret

B – Henry VIII and Anne Boleyn

C – Henry Tudor and Anne of Cleves

D – Charles I and Catherine Howard

Q3. Which of the following race car drivers is British?

A – Nico Rosberg

B – Sebastian Vettel

C – Jenson Button

D – Michael Schumacher

Q4. Why is Bonfire Night celebrated?

A – To celebrate the failure of the 1717 plot to blow up the Houses of Parliament

B – To celebrate the failure of Guy Fawkes's attempt to become King

C – To celebrate the discovery of fire

D – To celebrate the failure by a group of Catholics to kill King James

Q5. The names of any person who has been accused of a crime can be released by the press. True or false?

A – True

B – False

Q6. Which of the below statements is true?

A – Preventing paedophilia and fraud is high priority for British police chiefs.

B – Preventing smoking in public places is of high priority for British police chiefs.

Q7. Who is the head of the Commonwealth?

A – The UK Monarch

B – The Scottish Prime Minister

C – The Archbishop of Canterbury

D – A democratically elected minister, appointed by all of the member states

Q8. Which two of the following are criminal offences?

A – Selling alcohol to someone over the age of 18

B – Carrying a weapon for self-defence

C – Verbally abusing your neighbour

D – Parking in a disabled space, despite not being disabled

Q9. Who initiated the Habeas Corpus Act?

A – Charles I

B – Oliver Cromwell

C – Charles II

D – James II

Q10. Why is Oliver Cromwell negatively thought of in Ireland?

A – Cromwell brutally enforced his authority in Ireland, resulting in the deaths of thousands of people.

B – Cromwell's authority was never accepted by the Irish, who saw Charles I as the rightful king.

C – Cromwell was Scottish born, and therefore the Irish refused to accept him.

D – Cromwell was a poor leader, who spent lavishly on his own personal gain, whilst leaving his people to starve.

Q11. Isaac Newton is the author of *Mathematical Principles of Natural Philosophy*. True or false?

A – True

B – False

Q12. Which of the following statements is true?

A – Ben Nevis is the highest mountain in Wales.

B – Mount Snowdon is the highest mountain in Wales.

Q13. Which of the following statements is true?

A – The EU creates laws for European countries, and these are legally binding for member states.

B – The EU creates laws for European countries, but these are not legally binding for member states.

Q14. Important areas of the countryside are maintained and kept open by which of the following organisations?

A – Manchester City FC

B – The US Marines Corps

C – The National Trust

D – The National Society for the protection of country welfare

Q15. Which of the following statements is true?

A – At Christmas time, young children are taught that Father Christmas brings them presents on Christmas Eve.

B – At Christmas time, young children are taught that Leon Trotsky brings them presents on Christmas Eve.

Q16. Alfred Hitchcock directed which of the following films:

A – Lawrence of Arabia

B – The Killing Fields

C – Four Weddings and a Funeral

D – The 39 Steps

Q17. The patron saint of England is St Charles. True or false?

A – True

B – False

Q18. Scotland was the only one of the home nations who failed to qualify for Euro 2016. True or false?

A – True

B – False

Q19. Why do some historians view the Iron Age as the beginning of recorded British history?

A – The Iron Age produced the first historians, as people began to study their past.

B – The Iron Age was the first period of British history.

C – The people of the Iron Age created minted coins.

D – The people of the Iron Age created minted coins, inscribed with the names of kings.

Q20. The Statute of Rhuddlan attempted to establish English rule in Wales. True or false?

A – True

B – False

Q21. Why did the Glencoe Massacre take place?

A – The MacDonald clan of Glencoe were late for swearing fealty to William III.

B – The MacDonald clan of Glencoe were rude to William III whilst he was placing his order.

C – The MacDonald clan of Glencoe refused to yield to the power of William III.

D – The Glencoe clan of MacDonald refused to yield to the power of William III.

Q22. In the UK, once you have voted, your vote will be published online for everyone to see. True or false?

A – True

B – False

Q23. Which two of the following are common features of the small claims procedure?

A – These cases are heard before a judge and jury

B – These cases are heard before a judge, without a jury

C – These cases are heard in a small room, without lawyers

D – These cases are heard in a small room, with lawyers present

Q24. Which of the below statements is true?

A – Members of the School Board are responsible for making sure that the school adheres to and maintains high standards.

B – Members of the School Board are responsible for making sure that the school's R.E. programme incorporates the key religion of Christianity.

TEST 3

Q1. Which two countries have their patron saint's day as a public holiday?

A – England

B – Wales

C – Northern Ireland

D – Scotland

Q2. David Hockney was a huge contributor to which 1960s movement?

A – The punk movement

B – The pop art movement

C – The free love movement

D – The anti-authoritarian rap movement

Q3. At the Battle of Waterloo, the British forces led by the Duke of Wellington, defeated the French forces led by:

A – Nelson

B – Napoleon

C – Noakes

D – Ninkovich

Q4. Which of the following statements is true?

A – In 2007, Tony Blair was replaced as Prime Minister by Gordon Brown.

B – In 2007, Tony Blair was replaced as Prime Minister by David Cameron.

Q5. Which of the following is the most popular sport in the UK?

A – Wrestling

B – Darts

C – Cricket

D – Football

Q6. Which two of the following criteria are covered by employment law?

A – Disputes over wages

B – Faulty good and services

C – Eviction issues

D – Unfair dismissal

Q7. Every year, the Boat Race (a rowing event), takes place between which two of the following universities?

A – Oxford

B – Durham

C – Warwick

D – Cambridge

Q8. The total value of the Crown Jewels amounts to an estimated minimum of:

A – 100 billion pounds

B – 20 billion pounds

C – 1 million pounds

D – 6 million pounds

Q9. Henry VIII passed the Act of the Government of Wales. What was this?

A – An act that severed English ties with Wales, and made Wales its own independent country

B – An act that united England with Wales, and placed Welsh representatives in Parliament

C – An act that declared war on Ireland, on behalf of England and Wales

D – An act which ensured that Welsh rebellions would be punished mercilessly

Q10. What was the ultimate outcome of the English Civil War, for Charles I?

A – He was exiled to Scotland

B – He was betrayed by his own men, and murdered by a baying mob

C – He was defeated and executed by beheading

D – He was triumphant, and executed the Parliament usurpers

Q11. Who wrote the murder-mystery play, *The Mousetrap*?

A – Sherlock Holmes

B – Raymond Chandler

C – Agatha Christie

D – Richard McMunn

Q12. Andy Murray is only the second male British tennis player to have won a Grand Slam, since 1936. True or false?

A – True

B – False

Q13. The UN was set up after which of the following global events?

A – WWI

B – WWII

C – The Boer War

D – The Vietnam War

Q14. Which of the below statements is true?

A – In England, there are some counties which still use the death penalty.

B – England no longer uses the death penalty. Instead, criminals are sent to prison.

Q15. Which of the below statements is true?

A – As an intelligence agency, GCHQ works to repel the threat from extremist organisations such as Islamic State.

B – As an environmental agency, GCHQ works to ensure the protection of important environmental areas, such as the Eden Project.

Q16. Which two of the following are able to run for public office in the United Kingdom?

A – Members of the armed forces

B – Teachers

C – Civil servants

D – Paramedics

Q17. The Council of Europe is responsible for which of the following:

A – For ensuring that the laws surrounding human rights are respected and adhered to in its member countries

B – For ensuring that the laws surrounding fuel consumption are respected and adhered to in its member countries

C – For ensuring that the laws surrounding terrorism and conspiracy are respected and adhered to in its member countries

D – For ensuring that the laws surrounding consumerism are respected and adhered to in its member countries

Q18. Which of the following statements is true?

A – The satirical magazine *Punch* was published for the first time during the 1840s.

B – The satirical magazine *Punch* was published for the first time during the 1940s.

Q19. Which two of the following were wives of Henry VIII?

A – Mary Stuart

B – Emeline Pankhurst

C – Anne of Cleves

D – Catherine Parr

Q20. Along with Germany, which two countries actively participated in the annexation of areas of Czechoslovakia?

A – Poland and Hungary

B – Britain and Russia

C – Japan and France

D – USA and Italy

Q21. Which of the following statements is true?

A – Richard Austen Butler, a Labour MP, became responsible for education in 1941.

B – Howard Florey and Ernst Chain were the first scientists to work out how to use Penicillin as a medicine.

Q22. Which of the following statements is true?

A – Loch Ness is the largest lake in Scotland.

B – Loch Ness is the second largest lake in Scotland.

Q23. The White Tower, in the Tower of London, was built on the orders of which king?

A – Henry VIII

B – William the Conqueror

C – Richard III

D – King Gus

Q24. The annual Remembrance Day Service is held at The Cenotaph. True or false?

A – True

B – False

TEST 4

Q1. Which of the following statements is true?

A – One of the most important principles of The Enlightenment was that everyone should have the right to vote, and state their own political beliefs and views.

B – One of the most important principles of The Enlightenment was that everyone should have the right to their own political and religious beliefs.

Q2. The Union Flag consists of how many crosses?

A – 1

B – 2

C – 3

D – 4

Q3. Which of the below statements is true?

A – Driving your car to work in the morning is a good way of creating less pollution.

B – Taking the bus to work in the morning is a good way of creating less pollution.

Q4. The Loch Ness Monster has been scientifically proven to exist. True or false?

A – True

B – False

Q5. What is a constituency?

A – A small group of politicians

B – A small group of voters

C – A small area of the country

D – A county

Q6. The National Eisteddfod celebrates music, dance, art and other original performances. In which country is this held?

A – Scotland

B – Wales

C – Northern Ireland

D – England

Q7. Which of the below statements is true?

A – UK Law states that you must be at least 17 years old to drive a car, but 16 to drive a motorbike.

B – UK Law states that you must be at least 16 years old to drive a moped, but 17 to drive a motorbike.

Q8. Which TWO of the following are NOT members of the Commonwealth?

A – Rwanda

B – Italy

C – Afghanistan

D – India

Q9. Under Queen Victoria, Britain repealed the Corn Laws. What was the result of this?

A – It became easier to import cheap raw materials – such as grain – which in turn bolstered British industry.

B – It became harder to import cheap raw materials – such as grain – which in turn bolstered British industry.

C – Farmers suffered as they could no longer get fair prices for their grain, meaning many people were forced to move away from the countryside to survive.

D – Farmers flourished as they could now get fair prices for their grain, meaning that many people left the city and moved to the countryside to make more money.

Q10. Which of the following statements is true?

A – Anne Boleyn was Henry VIII's third wife. She was beheaded.

B – Jane Seymour was Henry VIII's third wife. She was divorced.

Q11. From which time period does the poem *Beowulf* originate?

A – Norman

B – Elizabethan

C – Stuart

D – Anglo-Saxon

Q12. Sir Robin Knox-Johnston was the first person to accomplish which of the following:

A – Running 900 miles without stopping

B – Sailing single-handed around the world, without stopping

C – Swimming 500 miles without shopping

D – Flying single-handed around the continent, without stopping

Q13. *The Golden Hand*, which belonged to Francis Drake, was one of the first ships to sail around the world. True or false?

A – True

B – False

Q14. Isambard Kingdom Brunel constructed which major transport means?

A – The M20

B – The London Underground

C – The Great Western Railway

D – The Orient Express

Q15. Where in England will you find Anfield Stadium?

A – Manchester

B – Liverpool

C – Kent

D – London

Q16. In the UK, Christians make up over half of the religious population. True or false?

A – True

B – False

Q17. Which of the following statements is true?

A – Ealing Studios has a claim to being the oldest continuously working film studio facility in the world.

B – Maidstone Studios has a claim to being the oldest continuously working film studio facility in the world.

Q18. What is the minimum age requirement to drive a car or motorcycle?

A – 17

B – 16

C – 21

D – 18

Q19. Which of the following statements is true?

A – The British used fighter planes such as the Spitfire and the Luftwaffe to repel German forces.

B – The British used fighter planes such as the Spitfire and the Hurricane to repel German forces.

Q20. Which of the following statements is true?

A – Julius Caesar was the first Roman leader to attempt an invasion of Britain.

B – Emperor Claudius was the first Roman leader to attempt an invasion of Britain.

Q21. The Grand National is a:

A – Annual parliamentary meeting

B – Novel by Charles Dickens

C – Horse race

D – Football stadium

Q22. In which country will you find the cities of Birmingham and Plymouth?

A – Scotland

B – Wales

C – England

D – Republic of Ireland

Q23. Snowdon is the highest point of which country?

A – Wales

B – Northern Ireland

C – England

D – Scotland

Q24. Which of the following statements is true?

A – The Welsh language is separate to English.

B – The Welsh language is very similar to English and the two are often mixed together.

TEST 5

Q1. England are the only country in Great Britain with an international football cup win to their name. True or false?

A – True

B – False

Q2. Which of the following landmarks is built upon Castle Rock, part of an ancient volcano?

A – Hever Castle

B – Leeds Castle

C – Windsor Palace

D – Edinburgh Castle

Q3. John Petts was an artist best known for his contributions to the field of abstract painting. True or false?

A – True

B – False

Q4. Which of the below statements is true?

A – Tax evasion in the UK is a serious offence.

B – Tax evasion in the UK is not treated as a serious offence.

Q5. Which of the below statements is true?

A – The UK police is a public service, but are biased towards the middle and upper classes.

B – The UK police is a public service, who are unbiased and protect everyone.

Q6. Which two of the following were among the terms of the Treaty of Versailles?

A – Germany had to accept total responsibility for the war.

B – Germany had to surrender to an American/British coalition rule.

C – Germany had to pay extensive reparation fees.

D – Germany had to allow the British people to vote in their national elections.

Q7. Which of the following statements is true?

A – Although Hadrian's Wall is not a UNESCO World Heritage Site, it remains extremely popular with walkers.

B – Hadrian's Wall is a UNESCO World Heritage Site, and remains extremely popular with walkers.

Q8. What is 'panto'?

A – A type of musical comedy, performed on stage.

B – A type of romantic drama, performed on TV.

C – A type of situational comedy, performed on TV.

D – A type of musical tragedy, performed on stage.

Q9. Like other TV channels, the BBC is funded through advertisements and subscriptions. True or false?

A – True

B – False

Q10. The European Convention on Human Rights was created by which of the following bodies?

A – NATO

B – The UN

C – The Council of Europe

D – The European Union

Q11. William Shakespeare was born in Kingston upon Thames. True or false?

A – True

B – False

Q12. The role of the Speaker is to keep order during parliamentary debates. How is the Speaker chosen?

A – By the Monarch

B – By the Prime Minister

C – By the public

D – By the other MPs

Q13. The practice of female genital mutilation in the UK is illegal. However, it is legal to take a woman abroad to have this done. True or false?

A – True

B – False

Q14. Every single member of the Commonwealth belongs to the British Empire. True or false?

A – True

B – False

Q15. With which country is the meal Ulster Fry traditionally associated?

A – England

B – Wales

C – Scotland

D – Northern Ireland

Q16. Towns and cities in the UK are governed by:

A – Gauleiters

B – NKVD

C – The Police and Crime Commissioner

D – Local authorities

Q17. Which of the following statements is true?

A – Working together, Britain and France produced the first supersonic commercial airliner.

B – Working together, Britain and Germany produced the first supersonic commercial airliner.

Q18. From 1853-1913, over 13 million people left Britain. True or false?

A – True

B – False

Q19. The Isle of Man is a:

A – Part of the UK

B – Irish settlement

C – Crown Dependency

D – Nature Reserve

Q20. Which of the following statements is true?

A – The Moderator of the General Assembly of the Church of Scotland is re-elected every 3 years.

B – The Moderator of the General Assembly of the Church of Scotland is appointed for one year only.

Q21. Thomas Chippendale is famous for:

A – Designing furniture

B – Painting portraits

C – Winning 5 tennis Grand Slams

D – Passing longstanding UK laws in Parliament

Q22. The responsibilities of Police and Crime Commissioners include:

A – Building relationships with medical surgeries around the UK

B – Ensuring that the public know where their local police station is

C – Patrolling the streets of the UK, to tackle crime

D – Setting the local policing budget

Q23. Which of the below statements is true?

A – Any man who forces a woman to have sex can be charged with rape, with the exemption being if they are the woman's husband.

B – Any man who forces a woman to have sex can be charged with rape, including the woman's husband.

Q24. In order to apply for a National Insurance Number, you will generally need to supply documents that prove your identity. True or false?

A – True

B – False

TEST 6

Q1. The London Eye is situated in which position on the River Thames?

A – The middle

B – The eastern bank

C – The south bank

D – The London Eye is not situated by the River Thames

Q2. The 'Divine Right of Kings' refers to the belief that the king has been chosen by God to rule. True or false?

A – True

B – False

Q3. What sparked the outbreak of World War I?

A – The assassination of Archduke Franz Ferdinand

B – Appeasement

C – The Treaty of Versailles

D – The Bolshevik Revolution

Q4. In 1940, much to the shock of the world, Germany conquered which major European power?

A – Italy

B – Britain

C – France

D – Japan

Q5. Which food is traditionally eaten on Shrove Tuesday?

A – Turkey

B – Pancakes

C – Strawberries and cream

D – Yorkshire puddings

Q6. Which of the below statements is true?

A – In England and Wales, the small claims procedure is used for claims that amount to £5,000 or less.

B – In Scotland and Northern Ireland, the small claims procedure is used for claims that amount to £5,000 or less.

Q7. Your National Insurance Number allows the government to track your National Insurance contributions. True or false?

A – True

B – False

Q8. Working people in the UK are required to pay income tax. What does this money go towards?

A – The National Lottery

B – Private medical institutes and law firms

C – Roads, education and other public services

D – Animal experimentation

Q9. Diwali is celebrated by both Sikhs and Hindus. True or false?

A – True

B – False

Q10. People commemorate the 11th November by:

A – Wearing daffodils and attending church services

B – Wearing poppies and having a two minutes silence

C – Praying and chanting the names of the dead

D – Giving each other gifts and presents

Q11. The Prime Minister of the UK is a member of the House of Lords. True or false?

A – True

B – False

Q12. Which of the following statements is true?

A – Wilfred Owen is the writer of *Anthem for Doomed Youth.*

B – Wilfred Owen is the writer of *The Tyger.*

Q13. The Confederation of British Industry (CBI) are an example of a:

A – Pressure group

B – Trade Union

C – Environmental agency

D – Hereditary Peers Association

Q14. The longest distance on the UK mainland is between John O'Groats and Gillingham, Medway. True or false?

A – True

B – False

Q15. Which two of the following forms of disputes, can be settled under civil law?

A – Housing disputes

B – Workplace safety disputes

C – Military tribunal disputes

D – Employment disputes

Q16. Which of the following statements is true?

A – The UK contains 17 national parks

B – The UK contains 15 national parks

Q17. During the Middle Ages, what changes took place within the judging profession?

A – Judges began to be chosen by merit.

B – Judges began to be chosen by how wealthy they were.

C – Judges began to be chosen according to their status in society.

D – Judges began to be chosen based on how much the king liked them.

Q18. Which of the following statements is correct?

A – In the UK, Christmas is celebrated on the 25th December.

B – In the UK, New Year's Day is celebrated on the 2nd of January.

C – In the UK, Saint George's Day is celebrated on the 17th July.

D – In the UK, Halloween is celebrated on the 13th April.

Q19. Which of the below statements is true?

A – By becoming a citizen of the UK, you agree to accept the values and beliefs laid out by the Church of England; as the official church of the country.

B – People of the UK have total religious freedom and are free to believe in whatever they wish.

Q20. It is a legal requirement for BBC radio and television broadcasts to be politically balanced. True or false?

A – True

B – False

Q21. If you are a newly qualified driver in Northern Ireland, what type of plate must you display on your car?

A – An L plate

B – A C plate

C – An R plate

D – An F plate

Q22. It is a legal requirement for each local authority to make its electoral register available for anyone to view?

A – True

B – False

Q23. What is the name for the period of political strife that occurred in Northern Ireland, beginning in the 1970s?

A – The Glorious Revolution

B – Operation Valkyrie

C – The Easter Rising

D – The Troubles

Q24. Proportional Representation is the name for the system by which MEPs are elected. True or false?

A – True

B – False

TEST 7

Q1. When a defendant is found guilty in Crown Court, which of the following individuals decides upon the penalty?

A – The prosecution

B – The defence

C – The judge

D – The jury

Q2. In 55BC, Julius Caesar conquered Britain. True or false?

A – True

B – False

Q3. Which of the following statements is true?

A – In 1933, Adolf Hitler was named President of Germany.

B – In 1933, Adolf Hitler was named Chancellor of Germany.

Q4. Which two of the following forms of offence, can be charged under criminal law?

A – Littering

B – Carrying a weapon

C – Swearing

D – Smoking in a public place

Q5. Which of the following statements is true?

A – The Domesday Book was introduced by William the Conqueror, after his invasion of 1066.

B – The Domesday Book was introduced by King John, after his nobles demanded it.

Q6. The Reform Act of 1832 increased the number of people who could vote. True or false?

A – True

B – False

Q7. Why was Hadrian's Wall constructed?

A – To stop foreign invaders from gaining entry to British soil

B – To ensure that the legacy of Emperor Hadrian was remembered

C – To defy those who said building such a wall was impossible

D – To keep out Scottish rebels, who were unhappy with the Roman invasion

Q8. Loch Ness is part of the Caledonian Canal. True or false?

A – True

B – False

Q9. Charlie Chaplin is famous for his part in which type of movies?

A – Romantic comedies

B – Horror movies

C – Silent movies

D – Musicals

Q10. Scottish courts can deliver a verdict of 'not proven'. In this instance, what happens to the defendant?

A – They are released

B – They are sentenced to death

C – They are re-tried

D – They are found guilty

Q11. Who opens the new parliamentary session each year?

A – The Prime Minister

B – The Speaker

C – The Monarch

D – The leader of the opposition

Q12. Cowes is famous for hosting sailing events. Whereabouts is Cowes located?

A – Scotland

B – Northern Ireland

C – Wales

D – The Isle of Wight

Q13. Which of the following statements is true?

A – You can participate in the National Lottery by buying a ticket from a shop.

B – You can participate in the National Lottery by sending the organisers a letter with your chosen numbers.

Q14. *Auld Lang Syne* was written by which Scottish poet?

A – Roger Redwool

B – Roger Burns

C – Robert Bryans

D – Robert Burns

Q15. Which of the following statements is true?

A – During the Bronze Age, people buried their dead in tombs called round barrows.

B – During the Bronze Age, people buried their dead in tombs called mausoleums.

Q16. Coronation Street, Eastenders and Emmerdale are all examples of which type of TV programme:

A – Comedy

B – Period drama

C – Soap

D – Reality TV

Q17. If you owe a significant amount of money to someone, but are unable to pay, it is common practice for them to take you to court. True or false?

A – True

B – False

Q18. In the 2012 Olympics, Mo Farah won gold in the 6,000 and 12,000 metre races. True or false?

A – True

B – False

Q19. How did James I deal with Irish religious rebellions?

A – By ruthlessly executing all of those who rebelled against the crown

B – By encouraging Protestants to form 'plantations' in the northern province of Ulster

C – By encouraging Catholics to form 'plantations' in the northern province of Ulster

D – By offering the rebels gold and land in exchange for accepting a new religion

Q20. The penalty for watching TV without a licence can be up to:

A – A fine of £1,000

B – 20 years in prison

C – Community service

D – Exile to Siberia

Q21. Which two of the following forms of income, will you need to pay tax on?

A – Employment wages

B – Pet insurance

C – Book deliveries

D – Pension money

Q22. Which of the following is a reason for Britain having tight border controls?

A – To prevent terrorists from entering the country

B – To ensure that the British population does not reach a certain level

C – To prevent fraud and paedophilia

D – To ensure that Britain remains 'British'

Q23. Which of the below statements is true?

A – Although steps have been taken to legalise same sex marriage, there is no official act which has done this yet

B – The Same Sex Marriage Act of 2013 made it legal for people of the same sex to marry

Q24. Which of the below statements is true?

A – Pay As You Earn is the name for the system where your income tax is automatically taken from your wages.

B – Pay As You Earn is the name for the system where your income tax is paid weekly into a government account.

TEST 8

Q1. In the UK, women receive the right to vote once they turn 21. Men can vote once they reach the age of 18. True or false?

A – True

B – False

Q2. Which of the below statements is true?

A – You will be legally penalised for failing to recycle.

B – You won't be legally penalised for failing to recycle, but your bin men can refuse to take your rubbish.

Q3. If you are arrested by the police, you will be taken directly to:

A – The hospital

B – The courtroom

C – The police station

D – The Gulag

Q4. Which of the following statements is true?

A – In Northern Ireland, the anniversary of the Battle of the Boyne is a public holiday.

B – In Northern Ireland, the anniversary of the Battle of the Boyne is not a public holiday.

Q5. Which of the below statements is true?

A – In the UK, keeping your garden clean and tidy is important, but does not come under 'British values'.

B – In the UK, keeping your garden clean and tidy is a great way of demonstrating 'British values'.

Q6. The UK government is formed by the party who wins the majority of:

A – Constituencies

B – MPs

C – Charity donations

D – European recommendations

Q7. A General Election is held every:

A – 5 years

B – 6 years

C – 10 years

D – 8 years

Q8. Which of the following charities works to protect the environment?

A – NASA

B – Greenpeace

C – The RSPCA

D – NSPCC

Q9. Which of the below statements is true?

A – In the UK, it is illegal to drink alcohol in public. You can be fined or arrested for breaking this law.

B – In the UK, it illegal to drink alcohol in public in some locations. You can be fined or arrested for breaking this law.

Q10. Which of the below statements is true?

A – If you own a car in the UK, you will be required to pay a bi-annual (two yearly) vehicle tax.

B – If you own a car in the UK, you will be required to pay an annual vehicle tax.

Q11. On average, girls leave school with better qualifications than boys. True or false?

A – True

B – False

Q12. How many MPs are appointed by the Prime Minister, to act as cabinet ministers?

A – 10

B – 5

C – 8

D – 20

Q13. Which of the following statements is true?

A – John O'Groats is located on the east coast of Wales.

B – John O'Groats is located on the north coast of Scotland.

Q14. Florence Nightingale first came to prominence during the Crimean War. True or false?

A – True

B – False

Q15. Which of the following statements is true?

A – The North Atlantic Treaty Organisation (NATO) was set up to repel the threat of Nazi Germany.

B – The first test of the British Atomic Bomb was named Operation Hurricane.

Q16. Where in Britain will you find Europe's longest dry ski slope?

A – Near Sandwich

B – Near Bromley

C – Near Barming

D – Near Edinburgh

Q17. It is against UK Law to treat a pet with cruelty or neglect. True or false?

A – True

B – False

Q18. The United Kingdom consists of England, Scotland, Wales and the Republic of Ireland. True or false?

A – True

B – False

Q19. What is the Commonwealth?

A – A group of countries who work together to ensure mutual power and influence in the world.

B – A group of countries who work to influence world events and ensure things work in their favour.

C – A group of countries who work together for the purposes of democracy and international development.

D – A group of foreign entities, also known as Reptiles, who work together in conflict with other influential groups.

Q20. Although Henry VIII created his own church, England remained Catholic until his death in 1547. True or false?

A – True

B – False

Q21. In 1066, the Battle of the Somme was fought between William of Normandy, and Harold Godwinson. True or false?

A – True

B – False

Q22. Sake Dean Mahomet introduced scissors as a tool to England. True or false?

A – True

B – False

Q23. The Industrial Revolution saw the development of which mass production process?

A – The Bessemer Process

B – The Bassinger Process

C – The Bellinger Process

D – The Borringer Process

Q24. The Gunpowder Plot was instigated by a group of disillusioned Protestants, who plotted to blow up the Houses of Parliament. True or false?

A – True

B – False

TEST 9

Q1. Who printed *The Canterbury Tales*?

A – Geoffrey Chaucer

B – William Caxton

C – Samuel Pepys

D – Henry Tudor

Q2. The Hundred Years War was fought between Britain and France. True or false?

A – True

B – False

Q3. On which bridge in London will you find a statue of a Boudicca, commemorating her efforts against the Romans?

A – Westminster Bridge

B – London Bridge

C – Tower Bridge

D – Goldengate Bridge

Q4. The Prime Minister of the UK can be forced to resign if the MPs in his party decide they need a change. True or false?

A – True

B – False

Q5. The distance from Land's End to John O'Groats is 870 miles. True or false?

A – True

B – False

Q6. London Fashion Week takes place three times a year. True or false?

A – True

B – False

Q7. Which of the following statements is true?

A – Roald Dahl was born in Wales

B – Roald Dahl was born in England

Q8. Which of the following statements is true?

A – The Highland Clearances was the name for the demolishing of small farms, to make space for livestock.

B – The Highland Clearances was the name for the demolishing of small farms, to make room for industrial factories.

Q9. Which of the following statements is true?

A – The Great Plague of 1666 was the worst epidemic of disease ever to hit Britain.

B – The Black Death of 1348 was the worst epidemic of disease ever to hit Britain.

Q10. During the Victorian Age, more than half of the world's iron, coal and cotton was produced by the UK. True or false?

A – True

B – False

Q11. NATO consists of which two of the following:

A – North American countries

B – South American countries

C – European countries

D – Middle Eastern countries

Q12. Which of the following statements is true?

A – The Normans brought feudalism to England.

B – The Anglo-Saxons brought feudalism to England.

Q13. Following the battle of Bosworth Field, Henry Tudor married which of the following women?

A – Margaret of Anjou

B – Anne of Cleves

C – Margaret Thatcher

D – Elizabeth of York

Q14. Harold Pinter is a previous winner of the Nobel Prize in Literature. True or false?

A – True

B – False

Q15. Who was William Wilberforce?

A – A pro-slavery campaigner

B – An anti-slavery campaigner

C – A British merchant

D – A slave

Q16. During the War of the Roses, the sigil of House York was a white rose. True or false?

A – True

B – False

Q17. Feudalism is the name for a system where farmers united their farms into one collective farm. True or false?

A – True

B – False

Q18. On the 1st April, which event is celebrated up until 12 midday?

A – April Fools

B – Valentines

C – Halloween

D – Easter

Q19. The patron saint of England is St Charles. True or false?

A – True

B – False

Q20. Which of the following is an overseas British territory?

A – Spain

B – Wales

C – Hawaii

D – The Falklands Islands

Q21. In the UK, you must be 21 years or older to participate in gambling. True or false?

A – True

B – False

Q22. The artist Inigo Jones designed which of the following?

A – The Banqueting House in Whitehall, London

B – The Globe Theatre in Southwark, London

C – St Paul's Cathedral on Ludgate Hill, London

D – The Etihad Stadium, Manchester

Q23. At present, there are more Jewish people than Hindu people in the UK. True or false?

A – True

B – False

Q24. V festival and the Isle of Wight festival are festivals of which kind?

A – Food

B – Music

C – Sport

D – Literature

TEST 10

Q1. Ian Fleming is the author of the well-known series, *Lord of the Rings*. True or false?

A – True

B – False

Q2. Sir Thomas Gainsborough was a famous British landscape painter. True or false?

A – True

B – False

Q3. Henry Moore is best known for:

A – Leading the England football team to victory in 1966

B – His ground-breaking architectural work

C – His abstract sculptures

D – His contributions to UK poetry

Q4. The expression 'bowled a googly' originates from which sport?

A – Football

B – Darts

C – Rounders

D – Cricket

Q5. If you are over the age of 75, then you are eligible to apply for a free TV licence. True or false?

A – True

B – False

Q6. Evelyn Waugh is best known for writing which of the following novels?

A – *The Return of the King*

B – *The Green Mile*

C – *Milly Molly Mandy*

D – *Brideshead Revisited*

Q7. What type of church is the national Church of Scotland?

A – Catholic

B – Protestant

C – Mormon

D – Presbyterian

Q8. Which sport does Dame Ellen MacArthur compete in?

A – Sailing

B – Tennis

C – Sprinting

D – Javelin

Q9. Colin Firth has never won an Oscar. True or false?

A – True

B – False

Q10. Which of the following statements is true?

A – Prior to Easter, Christians take a period of 40 days to reflect and prepare. This is known as Pent.

B – Prior to Easter, Christians take a period of 40 days to reflect and prepare. This is known as Lent.

Q11. Which of the following statements is true?

A – On Remembrance Day, people wear orchids on their jackets, as a sign of respect for those who died in World War I.

B – On Remembrance Day, people wear poppies on their jackets, as a sign of respect for those who died in World War I.

Q12. The Ashes is a series of cricket matches played between England and which country?

A – India

B – West Indies

C – Australia

D – Pakistan

Q13. What is the nickname for the huge bell outside of the Houses of Parliament?

A – Big Bong

B – Big Bill

C – Big Ben

D – Big Bell

Q14. The Crown Jewels are kept in Westminster Palace. True or false?

A – True

B – False

Q15. Alexander McQueen and Vivienne Westwood are leading brands in which industry?

A – The music industry

B – The food industry

C – The theatre industry

D – The fashion industry

Q16. While most offenders between the ages of 10-17 will be tried in a Youth Court, serious cases can result in a different trial. True or false?

A – True

B – False

Q17. In Scotland, a verdict of 'not guilty' will see the defendant walk away freely. However, 'not proven' means that they must be re-tried. True or false?

A – True

B – False

Q18. In the UK, domestic violence is a crime which can be prosecuted. Domestic violence can be defined as:

A – When a husband acts violently towards his wife

B – When a wife acts violently towards her husband

C – When any person acts violently towards their partner

D – When a man acts violently towards anyone

Q19. Which of the below statements is true?

A – Since 2012, England and Northern Ireland have had elected Police and Crime Commissioners.

B – Since 2012, England and Wales have had elected Police and Crime Commissioners.

Q20. Which of the below statements is true?

A – Britain played an essential role in the creation of the European Convention on Human Rights.

B – Although Britain did not play an essential role in the creation of the European Convention on Human Rights, it is now one of the strongest upholders of this convention.

Q21. It is a legal requirement for you to register your car with which of the following:

A – The local council

B – The UK government

C – The DVLA

D – The RSCPA

Q22. What is canvassing?

A – When a British artist decides to create a large, local canvas painting

B – When a member of a political party attempts to persuade others to support their candidate

C – When a member of a political party attempts to run for the role of Prime Minister

D – When UK volunteers group together to perform charitable acts and help the community

Q23. The modern Scottish parliament was formed in 1999. True or false?

A – True

B – False

Q24. Which of the following statements is true?

A – Chocolate eggs are given at Easter to celebrate the beginning of new life.

B – Chocolate eggs are given at Easter to celebrate Jesus's ascent to heaven.

TEST 11

Q1. Which of the following statements is true?

A – Eid al-Fitr is a Sikh festival, held to thank Allah for helping Sikhs to complete their fast.

B – Eid al-Fitr is a Muslim festival, held to thank Allah for helping Muslims to complete their fast.

Q2. Which of the following statements is true?

A – During Diwali, there is a famous celebration that takes place in the city of Leicester.

B – During Diwali, there is a famous celebration that takes place in the city of Ipswich.

Q3. Which of the following authors wrote both *Jude the Obscure* and *Far from the Madding Crowd*?

A – Thomas Hardy

B – Thomas Beckett

C – Thomas Matthews

D – Thomas O'Malley

Q4. If a game of Test Match cricket lasts for 5 days, the match is cancelled and the winner is the team that has the most runs. True or false?

A – True

B – False

Q5. Which of the following statements is true?

A – Father's Day takes place three Sundays before Easter.

B – Mother's Day takes place three Sundays before Easter.

Q6. What is the Scottish equivalent of a County Court?

A – High Court

B – Magistrates Court

C – Court in Session

D – Wimbledon

Q7. Even if you are suffering from a life-threatening illness, you are legally obligated to attend jury duty. True or false?

A – True

B – False

Q8. Which of the following statements is true?

A – Maiden Castle, which still exists today, is an example of a Roman settlement.

B – Maiden Castle, which still exists today, is an example of an Iron Age hill fort.

Q9. Which of the following statements is true?

A – Admiral Nelson died in combat during the Battle of Trafalgar.

B – Admiral Napoleon died in combat during the Battle of Trafalgar.

Q10. In 1851, the Great Exhibition opened in Hyde Park, Tottenham. True or false?

A – True

B – False

Q11. Which of the following has animator Nick Park won?

A – A Grammy

B – A BAFTA

C – An Oscar

D – The Champions League

Q12. There is a National horseracing museum in Newmarket, Suffolk. True or false?

A – True

B – False

Q13. The London Eye contains 32 capsules, which can carry up to 25 people. True or false?

A – True

B – False

Q14. The UN has a Security Council, consisting of how many members?

A – 8

B – 9

C – 20

D – 15

Q15. William Shakespeare wrote plays during the reign of:

A – Henry VIII

B – James II

C – Queen Victoria

D – Elizabeth I

Q16. Which of the following statements is true?

A – Richard III, of House York, was slain during the Battle of the Somme in 1485.

B – Richard III, of House York, was slain during the Battle of Bosworth Field in 1485.

Q17. Which of the following statements is true?

A – Henry VIII's son, Edward, was a devout Protestant.

B – Henry VIII's daughter, Mary, was a devout Protestant.

Q18. Which of the following statements is true?

A – Following their successful invasion of Britain, the Romans followed up by successfully conquering Scotland.

B – Following their successful invasion of Britain, the Romans tried and failed to conquer Scotland.

Q19. In the middle of the 19th century, Ireland suffered from which major disaster?

A – The Great Plague

B – Famine

C – Flooding

D – Ebola

Q20. The Union Jack consists of three crosses. The cross of St George, the cross of St Andrew and the cross of:

A – St Jack

B – St Paul

C – St Patrick

D – St Iker

Q21. Why were there tensions between the British government and their North American colonies?

A – The British government wanted to tax their North American colonies, who opposed this.

B – The North American colonies wanted to expand their overseas territory and have a say in ruling Britain.

C – The British government wanted to remove their colonies in North America as it was costing them money.

D – The North American colony leaders were taxing their people too heavily.

Q22. In 1721, Robert Walpole was named the very first British Prime Minister. True or false?

A – True

B – False

Q23. A 'rotten-borough' was the name for an area where the voting constituency was controlled by just one rich family. True or false?

A – True

B – False

Q24. Which of the following statements is true?

A – Following the defeat of the Vikings, many of the invaders remained in England, settling in an area known as Danesbridge.

B – Following the defeat of the Vikings, many of the invaders remained in England, settling in an area known as Danelaw.

TEST 12

Q1. Which of the following statements is true?

A – There is a statue of Boudicca on Westminster Bridge, to commemorate her efforts in keeping the Romans at bay.

B – There is a statue of Boudicca on London Bridge, to commemorate her efforts in keeping the Romans at bay.

Q2. Which of the following statements is true?

A – The Fort of Vindolanda is a part of The Tower of London.

B – The Fort of Vindolanda is a part of Hadrian's Wall.

Q3. D-Day is seen as significant, as it represented the beginning of the allies taking back key territories from Germany. True or false?

A – True

B – False

Q4. Who gave the speech, 'I have nothing to offer but blood, toil, tears and sweat'?

A – Adolf Hitler

B – Joseph Stalin

C – Grigory Zinoviev

D – Winston Churchill

Q5. Which of the following statements is true?

A – Many of the best-known poets are buried in Poet's Corner at Westminster Abbey.

B – Many of the best-known poets are buried in Poet's Corner at St Paul's Cathedral.

Q6. The 11th November 1918 is significant because this was the date that WWI ended. True or false?

A – True

B – False

Q7. In 1913, the British government implemented a bill that would allow for 'Home Rule' in Ireland.

A – True

B – False

Q8. Who did England fight against in the Boer War?

A – France

B – Russia

C – Netherlands

D – Germany

Q9. What was the Act of Union?

A – An act that created the Kingdom of Great Britain, and linked England and Northern Ireland together

B – An act that disestablished the link between Scotland and England

C – An act that created the Kingdom of Great Britain, and linked England and Wales together

D – An act that created the Kingdom of Great Britain, and linked England and Scotland together

Q10. How many children did Elizabeth I have?

A – 4

B – 3

C – 2

D – 0

Q11. Which of the below statements is true?

A – If you are a non-UK National looking for work, and have permission to work in the country, you'll need to telephone the department for workplace safety to obtain a National Insurance Number.

B – If you are a non-UK National looking for work, and have permission to work in the country, you'll need to telephone the department for work and pensions to obtain a National Insurance Number.

Q12. What does NSPCC stand for?

A – National Society for the Printers Copyright Corporation

B – National Society for the Protection of Costumed Clowns

C – National Society for the Protection of Criminal Corporations

D – National Society for the Prevention of Cruelty to Children

Q13. Where is the UK national anthem most commonly played?

A – During important national occasions

B – During school assemblies

C – At tennis matches

D – Whenever the Queen is present

Q14. Democracy is a system of government where all decisions are made by the Prime Minister and his cabinet. True or false?

A – True

B – False

Q15. What did the Chartists campaign for?

A – For women to be able to vote

B – For the voting age to be reduced

C – For every man to be allowed to vote

D – For the upper and middle classes to have a more decisive vote

Q16. The National Citizen Service programme is responsible for organising the community service for young people who have committed crimes. True or false?

A – True

B – False

Q17. Which of the following is NOT a common responsibility of a Police Community Support Officer?

A – Patrolling UK streets

B – Assisting Police Officers in their everyday work

C – Delivering community service lessons to prisoners

D – Working directly with the public to ensure the community is a safe place to live

Q18. Which of the following bodies investigates crime in the UK?

A – The armed forces

B – The office of political governance

C – The RSPCA

D – The police

Q19. Civil law does NOT cover debt issues. True or false?

A – True

B – False

Q20. Which of the below statements is true?

A – Although the UK does not have refuges for sufferers of domestic abuse, victims can contact services such as the Citizens Advice Bureau for help and support.

B – There are a number of refuges in the UK, designed to shelter sufferers of domestic abuse.

Q21. Which of the below statements is true?

A – The UK has a fairly high crime rate compared to the rest of the world.

B – The UK has a fairly low crime rate compared to the rest of the world.

Q22. Which of the following statements is true?

A – The British Pound is the oldest currency that is in use today.

B – The British Pound is one of the oldest currencies that is in use today.

Q23. Which of the following statements is true?

A – The Fenians advocated for complete Irish independence.

B – Charles Stuart Parnell advocated for complete Irish independence.

Q24. Which of the following statements is true?

A – The Battle of Agincourt was fought between Britain and France, during the Hundred Years War.

B – The Battle of Agincourt was fought between Britain and France, during the War of Independence.

TEST 13

Q1. Parliamentary proceedings are published in an official report, known as 'Hansard'. However, they are not shown on TV. True or false?

A – True

B – False

Q2. Which of the following statements is true?

A – George Frederick Handel was the composer of *Music of the Royal Fireworks.*

B – George Frederick Handel was the composer of *Peter Grimes.*

Q3. Which of the following statements is true?

A – The National Eisteddfod of Wales includes a number of competitions for Welsh poetry.

B – The National Eisteddfod of Wales primarily focuses on literature, and has little to do with poetry.

Q4. Which of the following statements is true?

A – Festival season in the UK takes place during the spring.

B – Festival season in the UK takes place during the summer.

Q5. Which of the following people was instrumental in defeating the Spanish Armada in 1588?

A – The Duke of Wellington

B – David Beckham

C – Sir Francis Drake

D – Tony Blair

Q6. Robert and George Stephenson were the father and son combination who pioneered which piece of technology?

A – The digital clock

B – The railway engine

C – The Concorde

D – The shotgun

Q7. The Battle of Hastings was fought between the forces of William of Normandy and Harald Hardrada. True or false?

A – True

B – False

Q8. Catherine of Aragon was Henry VIII's fifth wife. She was beheaded. True or false?

A – True

B – False

Q9. Why was 'Bloody Mary' nicknamed thusly?

A – She was nicknamed 'Bloody Mary' because of her harsh treatment towards Catholics.

B – She was nicknamed 'Bloody Mary' because it was rumoured that she drank blood.

C – She was nicknamed 'Bloody Mary' because of her harsh treatment towards Protestants.

D – She was nicknamed 'Bloody Mary' because she had severe haemophilia.

Q10. One of the central themes of Rudyard Kipling's work was that the British Empire was a negative influence. True or false?

A – True

B – False

Q11. The Paralympics have their origin in the work of Sir John Senior, who worked at the Stoke Mandeville hospital. True or false?

A – True

B – False

Q12. Membership of the Commonwealth is entirely voluntary. True or false?

A – True

B – False

Q13. Ellie Simmonds was the youngest member of the British team at the 2008 Paralympic games. True or false?

A – True

B – False

Q14. Which of the below statements is true?

A – The European Convention on Human Rights provides British citizens with the right to free speech.

B – The European Convention on Human Rights provides British citizens with the right to free travel.

Q15. Which of the following annual events showcases garden design from Britain and around the world?

A – The Tottenham Flower Show

B – The Buckinghamshire Flower Show

C – The Parkwood Flower Show

D – The Chelsea Flower Show

Q16. David Allan was a Scottish painter, who was best known for painting:

A – Portraits

B – Landscapes

C – Vehicles in transit

D – The weather

Q17. The UK operates with a free press, meaning that newspapers and media in the UK are free from government control. True or false?

A – True

B – False

Q18. Wimbledon is the only Grand Slam tennis tournament that is played on:

A – Grass

B – Clay

C – Hard courts

D – Straw

Q19. Judges preside over disputes between organisations and members of the public. True or false?

A – True

B – False

Q20. What does PCSO stand for?

A – Police Community Service Officer

B – Police Community Service Offender

C – Police Community Support Officer

D – Police Community Supervising Officer

Q21. Arranged marriage in the UK is illegal. True or false?

A – True

B – False

Q22. The UK has no written constitution. This is because:

A – The people in charge of Britain reserve the right to bend and change the rules, and a written constitution would prevent them from imposing their will on the people.

B – The British government sees a potential constitution as a negative, which would prevent them from doing their jobs.

C – Britain has never had any revolution or uprising which required the government to create a constitution.

D – A constitution would prevent those in charge from acting flexibly, and could cause issues such as inflation and famine.

Q23. A judge is a professional who is responsible for interpreting the law, and ensuring that trials run in a smooth and fair fashion. True or false?

A – True

B – False

Q24. The Last Night of the Proms is held at which famous venue?

A – The Etihad Stadium

B – Old Bailey

C – The Royal Hall of Orchestral Music

D – The Royal Albert Hall

TEST 14

Q1. Which of the following statements is true?

A – Nearly 10% of the population has a parent or grandparent born outside of the UK.

B – Nearly 12% of the population has a parent or grandparent born outside of the UK.

Q2. Which two of the following are reasons for the rapid increase of the UK population in recent years?

A – Better access to hard drugs

B – Longer life expectancy

C – Increased migration

D – Lower crime rate

Q3. How are civil servants appointed?

A – Via a public election

B – Via an application process

C – Via a series of physical tests

D – Via a series of obstacle courses

Q4. James II was a fierce Protestant. True or false?

A – True

B – False

Q5. Which city is the capital of Scotland?

A – Belfast

B – Edinburgh

C – Aberdeen

D – Glasgow

Q6. The BAFTAs are the British equivalents of the Oscars. True or false?

A – True

B – False

Q7. Which of the following statements is true?

A – The main bank of the UK is known as the Royal Bank of Scotland.

B – The main bank of the UK is known as the Bank of England.

Q8. Which of the following statements is true?

A – Northern Ireland contains people who speak Irish Gaelic, and people who speak English.

B – Northern Irish people only speak English.

Q9. When did the term 'Scotland' first start to be used?

A – When the people of the North united under one king, to repel the Anglo-Saxons

B – When the Scottish parliament was first created, with the intention of breaking from Britain.

C – When the people of the North united under one king, Kenneth Scotland.

D – When Scotland failed to qualify for Euro 2016.

Q10. What is the Bayeux Tapestry?

A – A tapestry commemorating the events of the Battle of Bosworth field

B – A tapestry commemorating the events of the Battle of Waterloo

C – A tapestry commemorating the events of the Battle of Hastings

D – A tapestry commemorating the events of the Battle of the Somme

Q11. George I relied heavily on his ministers during his reign, as he suffered from a disability. True or false?

A – True

B – False

Q12. Richard Arkwright was a barber who went on to improve the way in which factory machines produced materials. True or false?

A – True

B – False

Q13. In 1918, the right to vote was given to women who were over the age of:

A – 21

B – 26

C – 30

D – 18

Q14. At the end of the war, Hitler was arrested and put on trial for his war crimes. True or false?

A – True

B – False

Q15. The BAFTA awards are hosted by which of the following:

A – The British Academy of Film and Television Arts

B – The British Academy of Film and Television Actors

C – The British Acting and Television Academy

D – The Best Artists For Television Academy

Q16. *Lawrence of Arabia* (1962) was directed by David Lean. True or false?

A – True

B – False

Q17. Which of the following statements is true?

A – The Council of Europe has the power to make laws.

B – The Council of Europe does not have the power to make laws.

Q18. Which of the following poets wrote, *Home Thoughts From Abroad*?

A – James Edwards

B – Samuel J Kerringer

C – Samuel Pepys

D – Robert Browning

Q19. Which of the following statements is true?

A – Following the mega-tsunami of 6100BC, northern marshlands were turned into the English Channel.

B – Following the mega-tsunami of 6100BC, southern marshlands were turned into the English Channel.

Q20. Which of the following statements is true?

A – The New Stone Age lasted from the introduction of farming, until the first time that metal was used.

B – The New Stone Age lasted from the first time that metal was used, until the first time that electricity was used.

Q21. Following his victory at the Battle of Hastings, William followed up by swiftly conquering Wales and Scotland. True or false?

A – True

B – False

Q22. Robert Bruce defeated the English at which battle?

A – The Battle of Mayfield

B – The Battle of Sandwich

C – The Battle of Bannockburn

D – The Battle of Partick Thistle

Q23. Which of the following statements is true?

A – In 1922, Ireland split into two countries – Northern Ireland and Southern Ireland.

B – In 1922, Ireland split into two countries – Northern Ireland and the Irish Free State.

Q24. The first tennis club in England was founded in 1872, at which location?

A – Grimsby

B – Deal

C – Gloucestershire

D – Leamington Spa

TEST 15

Q1. Which of the following statements is true?

A – The Swinging Sixties was nicknamed after the liberal development of fashion, music and cinema.

B – The Swinging Sixties was nicknamed after the music of Charles Manson became known to the world.

Q2. Which of the following statements is true?

A – From 1979 till 1990, Britain was run by a Liberal Democrat government.

B – From 1979 till 1990, Britain was run by a Conservative government.

Q3. The Wars of the Roses were fought between the supporters of which two families?

A – The House of Chatham

B – The House of York

C – The House of Senacre

D – The House of Lancaster

Q4. The Eden Project was opened in:

A – 2002

B – 1998

C – 2001

D – 2004

Q5. Wembley Stadium is located in West London. True or false?

A – True

B – False

Q6. If you wish to visit the House of Commons, or the House of Lords, you can queue up outside the building. True or false?

A – True

B – False

Q7. How many members of Scottish Parliament are there?

A – 12

B – 79

C – 129

D – 110

Q8. Since 1999, hereditary peers have had the automatic right to attend the House of Lords. True or false?

A – True

B – False

Q9. The Chancellor of the Exchequer is responsible for which of the following:

A – UK food

B – UK military

C – UK economy

D – UK national security

Q10. Which of the following statements is true?

A – Chelsea FC have played two Champions League finals at Wembley Stadium, and won both.

B – FC Barcelona have played two Champions League finals at Wembley Stadium, and won both.

Q11. Henry Purcell was the organist at which famous Abbey?

A – Westminster Abbey

B – Coventry Abbey

C – Gillingham Abbey

D – St Paul's Abbey

Q12. Britain, Wales and Northern Ireland compete together as one national football team. True or false?

A – True

B – False

Q13. In modern day 2016, there is now nothing left of Hadrian's Wall. True or false?

A – True

B – False

Q14. What is Constitutional Monarchy?

A – A system where the monarch can pass particular actions or laws, regardless of whether parliament agree.

B – A system where the monarch cannot pass particular actions or laws if parliament don't agree.

C – A system where the monarch and parliament come to joint decisions on important matters.

D – A system where if the monarch and parliament disagree, the public vote on what decision is made.

Q15. Queen Victoria was the longest serving monarch in British history. True or false?

A – True

B – False

Q16. From which war did the Victoria Cross originate?

A – The Boer War

B – The Iraq War

C – World War I

D – The Crimean War

Q17. Which of the below statements is true?

A – In Scotland, minor criminal offences go to a Justice of the Peace Court.

B – In Scotland, minor criminal offences are dealt with in a Magistrate's Court.

Q18. Which of the below statements is true?

A – In England, you will not be able to find the numbers of local solicitor services in the *Yellow Pages.*

B – In England, you will be able to find the numbers of local solicitor services in the *Yellow Pages.*

Q19. If you are self-employed, you don't need to pay National Insurance contributions. True or false?

A – True

B – False

Q20. People who are selected for jury duty are selected based on:

A – Their choice of career

B – Their availability at the time of selection

C – Their age

D – Random selection from people on the electoral register

Q21. A Youth Court can contain up to 3 special magistrates. True or false?

A – True

B – False

Q22. If you are charged with murder in England, you will be tried in which of the following courts?

A – The Small Claims Court

B – The High Court

C – The Magistrates Court

D – The Justice of the Peace Court

Q23. Which of the below statements is true?

A – A solicitor is a type of lawyer, who will provide you with advice on legal issues.

B – A solicitor is a form of civil servant, who is assigned to collect unpaid taxes.

Q24. Which of the below statements is true?

A – In Scotland, the system used to deal with young offenders is known as the Young Offenders Aid System.

B – In Scotland, the system used to deal with young offenders is known as the Children's Hearing System.

TEST 16

Q1. Which of the below statements is true?

A – England and Wales do not distinguish between the ages of offenders, and every offender will be subjected to the same type of court/trial.

B – England and Wales distinguish between the ages of offenders, and people of different ages will be subjected to different types of court/trial.

Q2. Which of the below statements is true?

A – In Northern Ireland, a system of youth conferencing is used to decide how child offenders should be dealt with.

B – In Northern Ireland, a system of trial by combat is used to decide how child offenders should be dealt with.

Q3. The UK police have a duty to do which of the following:

A – To ensure that citizens of the UK feel safe, protected and free from disturbance to their daily lives.

B – To ensure that citizens of the UK feel safe, protected and able to voice their opinions to the government.

Q4. In the UK, it is illegal to buy alcohol from a shop for anyone under the age of:

A – 18

B – 21

C – 20

D – 17

Q5. Manchester and Cardiff are both capitals of countries in the UK. True or false?

A – True

B – False

Q6. The Eden Project, which houses plants from all over the world, is located in Cornwall, England. True or false?

A – True

B – False

Q7. The Proms lasts 8 weeks, and celebrates which of the following:

A – Football

B – Rock music

C – Poetry

D – Orchestral music

Q8. Sir Arthur Conan Doyle was a pioneer in which genre of fiction?

A – Erotica

B – Detective

C – Gothic

D – Fantasy

Q9. In Scotland, the 2nd January is a public holiday. True or false?

A – True

B – False

Q10. In which year was the voting age changed from 21 to 18?

A – 1950

B – 1951

C – 1969

D – 1962

Q11. Women make up approximately what proportion of the UK workforce?

A – Half

B – One eighth

C – One third

D – Two thirds

Q12. Which of the following statements is true?

A – In the UK, more men than women study at university.

B – In the UK, more women than men study at university.

Q13. Which of the following statements is true?

A – In the UK, you will find women working in all sectors of the economy.

B – In the UK, there is a strong imbalance in the careers that men and women can achieve.

Q14. The Eden Project, in Cornwall, is home to which of the following:

A – Insects and exotic animals

B – Nuclear waste disposal factories

C – Global environmental group headquarters

D – Greenhouses and plants

Q15. The National Anthem of the UK starts with which of the following words:

A – God rest our gracious King

B – God bless our gracious Queen

C – Long live our noble King

D – God save our gracious Queen

Q16. MPs have a responsibility to do which TWO of the following:

A – To represent the people of their constituency in Parliament

B – To act as the speaker in the House of Commons

C – To fight strongly against opposing political parties

D – To discuss critical national issues

Q17. In which theatre were Shakespeare's plays performed?

A – The Hammersmith Apollo

B – The West End Theatre

C – The Royal Albert Hall

D – The Globe Theatre

Q18. Under Queen Victoria, Britain became the largest empire in history. True or false?

A – True

B – False

Q19. During the Crimean War, Britain was allied with which countries?

A – Russia and France

B – Russia and Turkey

C – France and Turkey

D – Russia and Holland

Q20. Which of the following statements is true?

A – In 1833, the Emancipation Act completely abolished slavery of any kind in the British Empire.

B – In 1833, the Emancipation Act completely abolished slavery of any kind in England, Northern Ireland, Scotland and Wales.

Q21. Which of the following statements is true?

A – The First World War ended at 11:30am on the 11th November 1918.

B – The First World War ended at 11am on the 11th November 1918.

Q22. Britain became a member of the EU in 1973, but left in 2014. True or false?

A – True

B – False

Q23. Who of the following is a famous British film director?

A – Ridley Scott

B – Martin Scorsese

C – James Cameron

D – Sir Chris Hoy

Q24. In the UK, the role of a jury is to do which of the following:

A – Decide on whether the person is guilty or not guilty

B – Decide on how long the sentence should be

C – Decide on whether the person should be put to death

D – Decide on which judge is best suited for the case

TEST 17

Q1. The Northern Ireland Assembly can be suspended at the behest of the UK Government. True or false?

A – True

B – False

Q2. In UK politics, what is the correct name for the second-largest party, at any given time?

A – The shadow cabinet

B – The cabinet

C – The Labour Party

D – The opposition

Q3. Complaints to the police can only be made by writing directly to the Chief Constable of your local station. True or false?

A – True

B – False

Q4. In the UK, the police are independent of the government. True or false?

A – True

B – False

Q5. The Magna Carta of 1215, established which key principle?

A – That the king could do as he pleased

B – That the king's noblemen had more power than him

C – That the king was subject to law, and had to consult with his noblemen to make key decisions

D – That the king was subject to law, but could still make key decisions without consulting with his noblemen

Q6. Which geographical event caused the creation of the English Channel?

A – The eruption of super volcanos on the Canary Islands

B – A mega-tsunami

C – Global warming

D – The Thames River bursting its banks

Q7. In 2012, the Queen celebrated which anniversary?

A – Her 42nd birthday

B – Her Diamond Jubilee (60 years as queen)

C – Her 10th year of marriage to Prince Philip

D – Her execution of Bolshevik rebels

Q8. Which of the following statements is true?

A – Mary Queen of Scots was executed on the orders of her sister, Queen Elizabeth I.

B – Mary Queen of Scots was executed on the orders of her cousin, Queen Elizabeth I.

Q9. Which of the following statements is true?

A – The Peasant's Revolt of 1381 was a result of feudalism.

B – The Peasant's Revolt of 1381 was a result of collectivisation.

Q10. Which of the following statements is true?

A – The Great Fire of London started at a bakery on Pudding Lane.

B – The Great Fire of London started at a candlestick shop on Pudding Lane.

Q11. Prime Minister's Questions, takes places how often?

A – Once every day

B – Once every week

C – Once every 3 months

D – Once every 6 months

Q12. In Scotland, the small claims procedure is used to settle claims of under £5,000. True or false?

A – True

B – False

Q13. What is the title of the National Anthem of the UK?

A – God Save Jerusalem

B – Rule Britannia

C – God Save the Queen

D – England's Green and Promised Land

Q14. It is a criminal offence to harass someone because of their ethnicity. True or false?

A – True

B – False

Q15. Youth Courts deal with individuals who are aged between 10 and 21 years old. True or false?

A – True

B – False

Q16. Every year, the Electoral Register is updated. This takes place during:

A – September or October

B – February or March

C – November or December

D – June or July

Q17. Which of the following statements is true?

A – Phil Taylor is the most successful racing driver of all time.

B – Phil Taylor is the most successful darts player of all time.

Q18. Which of the following statements is true?

A – Mo Farah was born in West London. He is a long distance ruuner and Olympic champion.

B – Mo Farah was born in Somalia. He is a long distance runner and Olympic champion.

Q19. Which of the following statements is true?

A – Video gaming is extremely popular in the UK.

B – Video gaming is not very popular in the UK.

Q20. What is a hill fort?

A – A small gated house, built on top of a hill

B – A well defended castle, built on top of a hill

C – A well defended settlement, built on top of a hill

D – An open settlement, where travellers could rest on their journeys

Q21. The Elizabethan Religious Settlement required any public or church officer member to swear allegiance to which monarch?

A – Henry VIII

B – Elizabeth I

C – Elizabeth II

D – Mary Queen of Scots

Q22. Which of the following statements is true?

A – Robert Burns was nicknamed 'The Bard'

B – Robert Burns was nicknamed 'The Muse'

Q23. Historians are unanimously agreed that the Suffragettes helped the cause of women's votes. True or false?

A – True

B – False

Q24. Why did Huguenots come to Britain?

A – To escape from religious persecution in their own countries

B – To discover whether the streets of London were really 'paved with gold'

C – To enforce their faith on the residents of the UK

D – To escape the famine that had spread across their own countries

TEST 18

Q1. Towns and cities in the UK are governed by which of the following:

A – A government elected council, selected by MPs and the Prime Minister

B – A democratically elected council, selected by the people living in the area

Q2. The House of Commons is formed by which of the following?

A – Elected MPs

B – Wealthy businessmen/women

C – The Prime Minister and his cabinet

D – Democratically elected elder statesmen

Q3. Which of the following statements is true?

A – Approximately 21% of the British population identify themselves as atheist.

B – Approximately 30% of the British population identify themselves as atheist.

Q4. Which of the following statements is true?

A – Only the Prime Minister has the right to select the Archbishop of Canterbury.

B – The Monarch of the UK has the right to select the Archbishop of Canterbury.

Q5. Which of the following statements is true?

A – The Church of Scotland is governed by ministers and elders.

B – The Church of Scotland is governed by the Archbishop of Canterbury.

Q6. The Women's Franchise League aimed to give married women better employability rights. True or false?

A – True

B – False

Q7. Which of the following statements is true?

A – The Glorious Revolution was named thusly, because of the lack of bloodshed that it involved.

B – The Glorious Revolution was named thusly, because William of Orange overthrew James II – a tyrannical king.

Q8. The mayor of a town acts as the leader of:

A – The UK

B – The police

C – The local council

D – The transport commission

Q9. The UK has always had a democratic voting system. True or false?

A – True

B – False

Q10. If you are setting up as self-employed, you won't need a National Insurance Number. True or false?

A – True

B – False

Q11. Youth Court cases are often heard by a district judge. True or false?

A – True

B – False

Q12. You will not have to pay a fee to gain entrance to the public galleries in the House of Commons and the House of Lords. True or false?

A – True

B – False

Q13. The Queen plays a leading role in which of the following:

A – Political changes in the UK

B – The UK TV schedule

C – Acting as an ambassador for the UK

D – Deciding who will sit in the House of Commons

Q14. In the UK, women can be prosecuted for being violent towards their romantic partner. True or false?

A – True

B – False

Q15. Gaelic is still spoken in:

A – Wales

B – England

C – Scotland

D – The Falklands Islands

Q16. Which of the following statements is true?

A – Stand-up comedy is a type of comedy where a comedian stands up and records themselves telling jokes in front of a camera.

B – Stand-up comedy is a type of comedy where a comedian stands up and talks to a live audience.

Q17. Which of the following statements is true?

A – The BBC is the largest broadcaster in the entire world.

B – The BBC is not the largest broadcaster in the entire world.

Q18. Which of the following statements is true?

A – Gilbert and Sullivan wrote comic operas, such as *HMS Pinafore* and *The Mikado.*

B – Gilbert and Sullivan wrote the music for shows such as *Jesus Christ Superstar* and *Evita.*

Q19. In which circumstance would a by-election take place?

A – In the event that the current MP of a constituency resigns/is unable to continue with the role

B – In the event that the current MP of a constituency is unable to prove themselves loyal to the regime

C – In the event that the current MP of a constituency wishes to replace their cabinet

D – In the event that the current MP of a constituency does not agree with the result of the parliamentary elections

Q20. The House of Commons has the power to overrule the House of Lords. True or false?

A – True

B – False

Q21. The UK government has been forced to suspend the Northern Irish Parliament in the past. True or false?

A – True

B – False

Q22. Following WWII, who succeeded Winston Churchill as Prime Minister?

A – David Lloyd George

B – Clement Atlee

C – Harry Truman

D – Roger Walpole

Q23. The 19th century Irish famine left many people with a feeling of resentment towards the British government. True or false?

A – True

B – False

Q24. Which of the following statements is true?

A – Hans Holbein was a painter in the 16th century. He was born and painted in Britain.

B – Hans Holbein was a painter in the 16th century. He was born abroad, but painted in Britain.

TEST 19

Q1. England, Wales, Scotland and Northern Ireland all have their own established churches. True or false?

A – True

B – False

Q2. Which two of the following are denominations of British currency?

A – 10p

B – 60p

C – 90p

D – 20p

Q3. Which of the below statements is true?

A – Members of the public cannot attend youth courts.

B – Members of the public are able to attend youth courts, in special circumstances.

Q4. Which of the below statements is true?

A – It is illegal to sell tobacco products to anyone under the age of 16 in the UK.

B – It is illegal to sell tobacco products to anyone under the age of 18 in the UK.

Q5. Which of the below statements is true?

A – In the UK, it is illegal to cause offence to someone based on the colour of their skin, excluding instances where the person is of white British origin.

B – In the UK, it is illegal to cause offence to someone based on the colour of their skin, with no exceptions.

Q6. Voluntary work has little benefit to the community, and should be performed to benefit the individual undertaking the work. True or false?

A – True

B – False

Q7. The members of the House of Lords are known as 'peers'. True or false?

A – True

B – False

Q8. In which sport did Sir Bobby Moore compete?

A – Tennis

B – Snooker

C – Rugby

D – Football

Q9. Both parents take equal responsibility for their children in a marriage. True or false?

A – True

B – False

Q10. There are usually two police constabularies for each area of the country. True or false?

A – True

B – False

Q11. Which of the following takes place three Sundays before Easter?

A – Mother's Day

B – Father's Day

C – Lent

D – April Fool's Day

Q12. In the UK, the government are able to interfere with the outcome of a trial. True or false?

A – True

B – False

Q13. Both Scotland and England use the same system to judge young people. True or false?

A – True

B – False

Q14. Who was Aneurin Bevan?

A – The Minister for Health under Clement Atlee

B – The judge of the Nuremberg War Trials

C – The first female Prime Minister

D – The leader of the Opposition during WIII

Q15. In the UK, the right to a fair trial is available to:

A – Everyone except whistle-blowers and murderers

B – Everyone except paedophiles

C – Everyone except murderers

D – Everyone

Q16. Although it is illegal to distribute and sell drugs such as heroin and ecstasy, it is not illegal to buy them. True or false?

A – True

B – False

Q17. Julian Barnes, Ian McEwan and Hilary Mantel are all past winners of which prestigious prize?

A – The Turner Prize

B – The Man Booker Prize

C – The Balon d'or

D – The Teen Choice Awards

Q18. Which of the following statements is true?

A – Religiously, Easter marks the day on which Jesus Christ died.

B – Religiously, Easter marks the day on which Jesus Christ rose from the dead.

Q19. Which of the following statements is true?

A – The day before Lent starts, is known as Shrove Tuesday.

B – The day before Lent starts, is known as Bolshevik Wednesday.

Q20. Which of the following statements is true?

A – *Sir Gawain and the Green Knight* tells the story of a footballer from Merseyside.

B – *Sir Gawain and the Green Knight* tells the story of one of the knights at the court of King Arthur.

Q21. How much discount do blind people receive off the cost of their TV licence?

A – 25%

B – 10%

C – 75%

D – 50%

Q22. Sir Francis Chichester and his crew were the first people to sail around the world. True or false?

A – True

B – False

Q23. Which of the following statements is true?

A – England, Scotland and Northern Ireland all use the same form of banknotes.

B – Scotland and Northern Ireland use different forms of banknotes to England.

Q24. Which of the following statements is true?

A – In the UK, Christmas is traditionally celebrated by eating turkey.

B – In the UK, Christmas is traditionally celebrated by eating lamb and beef.

TEST 20

Q1. Which of the following statements is true?

A – Bank holidays in the UK have religious significance.

B – Bank holidays in the UK have no religious significance.

Q2. Which of the following statements is true?

A – Frank Lauder directed *The Belles of St Trinians* (1954).

B – Frank Lauder directed *Don't Look Now* (1973).

Q3. Which of the following statements is true?

A – The Turner Prize was named after Joseph Turner, an influential landscape artist.

B – The Turner Prize was named after Bill Turner, an influential architect.

Q4. The system in which MPs are elected is known as:

A – Trial by combat

B – First past the post

C – First past the pole

D – First past the pins

Q5. The Prime Minister of the UK lives in 20 Downing Street. True or false?

A – True

B – False

Q6. Police officers in the UK are also tasked with participating in local schemes and initiatives, to benefit community wellbeing. True or false?

A – True

B – False

Q7. Which of the following sports originated in Scotland?

A – Cricket

B – Tennis

C – Skiing

D – Golf

Q8. Which of the below statements is true?

A – If you are a non-UK national looking for work, then you will need a National Insurance Number.

B – If you are a non-UK national looking for work, then you won't need a National Insurance Number, but you will need a work identification number.

Q9. Which of the below statements is true?

A – If you are working under the employment of someone else, your income tax will be paid directly to HMRB.

B – If you are working under the employment of someone else, your income tax will be paid directly to HMRC.

Q10. If you want to talk to an MP about a particular issue that concerns you, what should you do?

A – Ring them via their personal telephone number

B – Visit their house to speak to them in person

C – Attend the public gallery at the House of Commons

D – Attend a local surgery session

Q11. Volunteers are paid for the work that they do. True or false?

A – True

B – False

Q12. The House of Commons generally acts more independently from the government than the House of Lords. True or false?

A – True

B – False

Q13. The Scottish Parliament meets at Balmoral, to discuss key critical national issues. True or false?

A – True

B – False

Q14. Which of the below statements is true?

A – In the UK, when you die, it is mandatory for you to donate your organs to those who need them.

B – In the UK, when you die, it is optional for you to donate your organs to those who need them.

Q15. Which of the below statements is true?

A – You must be aged 16-70 to take part in jury duty.

B – You must be aged 18-70 to take part in jury duty.

Q16. Which of the below statements is true?

A – The British Red Cross is a charity which aims to help people suffering from crisis.

B – HMRC is a government funded charity which helps people decide what to do with their savings.

Q17. If you suspect or know that someone is being forced into a marriage without consent, you can apply for protection orders on their behalf. True or false?

A – True

B – False

Q18. At Christmas, people traditionally give chocolate eggs as presents. True or false?

A – True

B – False

Q19. In England, you will need to bring photographic identification with you in order to vote. True or false?

A – True

B – False

Q20. If you feel that someone is trying to persuade you to join an extremist group, what should you do?

A – Ignore them

B – Sign up immediately

C – Contact the government

D – Contact the police

Q21. Which of the below statements is true?

A – Failing to pay enough National Insurance Contribution will result in you being unable to receive benefits such as discounts on your motor insurance, and discounts on your television licence.

B – Failing to pay enough National Insurance Contribution will result in you being unable to receive benefits such as a full retirement pension, or being unable to claim Jobseeker's Allowance.

Q22. Which of the below statements is true?

A – Court orders can be obtained to protect a person from being forced into a marriage, or to protect a person in a forced marriage.

B – Court orders cannot be obtained to protect a person from being forced into a marriage, as this is the job of the police.

Q23. It is illegal for the Monarch of the UK to give the Prime Minister political advice. True or false?

A – True

B – False

Q24. If you have a driving licence that has been obtained in France, you will be eligible to use this in the UK for a period of:

A – 3 years

B – 12 months

TEST 21

Q1. Police officers are not required to follow the laws that they uphold. True or false?

A – True

B – False

Q2. Which of the below statements is true?

A – It is a criminal offence to drive without motor insurance in the UK.

B – It is not a criminal offence to drive without motor insurance in the UK, but you can be fined.

Q3. Which of the below statements is true?

A – Although Britain is one of the most liberal countries in the world, it still has a long way to go in order to catch up with other nations.

B – Britain is one of the most liberal countries in the world, and frequently sets a good example to other nations.

Q4. Which of the below statements is true?

A – The UK is a high priority for terrorist organisations, as it is a rich, western country.

B – The UK is a high priority for terrorist organisations, as it has a history of religious and human rights violations.

Q5. Which of these statements is true?

A – The term MEP stands for Member of the European Parliament.

B – The term MEP stands for Member of the English Parliament.

Q6. Civil law is used to settle disputes between which of the following:

A – Individuals and groups

B – The government and multi-national corporations

C – The government and the media

D – The police and the government

Q7. If you wish to make a complaint about the police in Northern Ireland, then you can contact which of the following?

A – The Prime Minister

B – Visiting the home of your local police sergeant

C – The Police Ombudsman

D – The Independent Police Complaints Commission

Q8. Which of the below statements is true?

A – If you are self-employed, then you will need to pay your own National Insurance Contributions, via a system called 'self-assessment'.

B – If you are self-employed, then you will need to pay your own National Insurance Contributions, via a system called 'self-tax declaration'.

Q9. Which of the below statements is true?

A – In the UK, all young people are provided with a National Insurance number just before their 17th birthday.

B – In the UK, all young people are provided with a National Insurance Number just before their 16th birthday.

Q10. The members of the House of Commons are elected democratically. True or false?

A – True

B – False

Q11. Under Queen Victoria, Britain made changes to which of the following working laws?

A – Providing workers with the means to rise up and overthrow factory managers

B – Giving workers better on-site food and drinks access

C – Reducing the number of hours that women and children could work per day

D – Ensuring that all staff had proper medical training to deal with on-site

Q12. In 1929, which negative event occurred, impacting countries all over the world?

A – World War II

B – The Great Depression

C – The attack on the Twin Towers

D – The Indonesian Tsunami

Q13. Which of the below statements is true?

A – If you are embroiled in a legal dispute, or have been charged with a crime, you can hire a solicitor.

B – If you are embroiled in a legal dispute, or have been charged with a crime, you can hire a policeman.

Q14. Which of the below statements is true?

A – Hiring a solicitor in the UK is free of charge, as they are funded entirely by the government.

B – Hiring a solicitor in the UK can be expensive, and incur significant legal costs.

Q15. Florence Nightingale is seen by many people as the founder of modern nursing. True or false?

A – True

B – False

Q16. You must be of which minimum age in order to run for public office:

A – 16

B – 18

C – 19

D – 28

Q17. Which two of the following countries compete in the Six Nations Rugby Championship?

A – Zimbabwe

B – South Africa

C – Italy

D – France

Q18. Which of the following statements is true?

A – John Milton is the author of *Paradise Lost.*

B – Graham Greene is the author of *Paradise Lost.*

Q19. Charles Stuart Parnell campaigned for Ireland to separate completely from the UK. True or false?

A – True

B – False

Q20. Which of the below statements is true?

A – If you have experienced domestic abuse, you can contact the Citizens Advice Bureau for guidance.

B – If you have experienced domestic abuse, you can contact the RSCPA for guidance.

Q21. Who wrote the *Just So* stories?

A – John Hunter

B – Hermann Goering

C – Nikolai Bukharin

D – Rudyard Kipling

Q22. Which of the below statements is true?

A – Individual police constabularies are headed by chief constables.

B – Individual police constabularies are headed by police and crime commissioners.

Q23. Which of the below statements is true?

A – At present, the biggest threat to the United Kingdom is from the so-called Islamic State; and other like-minded organisations.

B – At present, the biggest threat to the United Kingdom is from political dissenters within the country, who seek to overthrow the government.

Q24. Small claims are able to be issued online. True or false?

A – True

B – False

ANSWERS TO TESTS
(1-21)

Test 1

Q1. Members of the Northern Ireland Assembly meet in Belfast. True or false?

Answer: A – True

Q2. If you are unable to vote in person, then you can submit your vote via:

Answer: D – Post

Q3. The role of the Home Secretary is to:

Answer: B – Manage the country's security services

Q4. During the Bronze Age, people lived in what became known as 'bronze houses'. True or false?

Answer: B – False

Q5. St Augustine was rewarded for his missionary efforts by being made Archbishop of Canterbury. True or false?

Answer: A – True

Q6. Which of the following statements is true?

Answer: A – One of the negative sides to the Industrial Revolution was the poor working conditions, where there were very few laws in place to protect employees.

Q7. How many people sit on a jury in England?

Answer: D – 12

Q8. Once you reach the age of 70, you will need to renew your driving licence every:

Answer: C – 3 years

Q9. During the Civil War, the supporters of King Charles I were known as 'the Roundheads'. True or false?

Answer: B – False

Q10. Who was the author of *The Jungle Book*?

Answer: B – Rudyard Kipling

Q11. Why does the Welsh dragon not appear on the Union Flag?

Answer: C – Wales was already united with England when the Union Flag was created.

Q12. Sir William Walton was the composer of which of the following:

Answer: D – Belshazzar's Feast

Q13. Which two of the following are plays written by William Shakespeare:

Answer: A – Romeo and Juliet, C – The Taming of the Shrew

Q14. In 1348, which of the following diseases arrived in England?

Answer: B – The Black Death

Q15. Who deals with complaints about the police in Scotland?

Answer: B – The Police Complaints Commissioner

Q16. Which of the below statements is true?

Answer: A – The National Citizen Service provides 16-17 year olds with the chance to develop their skills and take part in community schemes.

Q17. Which two of the following are security services operating in the UK, to prevent crime and terrorism?

Answer: B – MI5, D – GCHQ

Q18. Which national flower is commonly associated with Scotland?

Answer: C – The Thistle

Q19. The Falklands Islands are a part of the UK. True or false?

Answer: B – False

Q20. During your citizenship ceremony, you will have to recite which of the following:

Answer: B – The oath of allegiance

Q21. Damien Hirst and Richard Wright are both winners of which prestigious award?

Answer: A – The Turner Prize

Q22. You can be ruled out of participating in jury duty, if:

Answer: D – You have certain criminal convictions

Q23. Which of the following statements is true?

Answer: A – Boxing Day is a public holiday in the UK.

Q24. What did the suffragettes campaign for?

Answer: A – The right for women to vote

Test 2

Q1. Which of the following poets wrote *She Walks In Beauty*?

Answer: C – Lord Byron

Q2. Elizabeth I was the daughter of:

Answer: B – Henry VIII and Anne Boleyn

Q3. Which of the following race car drivers is British?

Answer: C – Jenson Button

Q4. Why is Bonfire Night celebrated?

Answer: D – To celebrate the failure by a group of Catholics to kill King James

Q5. The names of any person who has been accused of a crime can be released by the press. True or false?

Answer: B – False

Q6. Which of the below statements is true?

Answer: A – Preventing paedophilia and fraud is high priority for British police chiefs.

Q7. Who is the head of the Commonwealth?

Answer: A – The UK Monarch

Q8. Which two of the following are criminal offences?

Answer: B – Carrying a weapon for self-defence, D – Parking in a disabled space, despite not being disabled

Q9. Who initiated the Habeas Corpus Act?

Answer: C – Charles II

Q10. Why is Oliver Cromwell negatively thought of in Ireland?

Answer: A – Cromwell brutally enforced his authority in Ireland, resulting in the deaths of thousands of people.

Q11. Isaac Newton is the author of Mathematical Principles of Natural Philosophy. True or false?

Answer: A – True

Q12. Which of the following statements is true?

Answer: B – Mount Snowdon is the highest mountain in Wales.

Q13. Which of the following statements is true?

Answer: A – The EU creates laws for European countries, and these are legally binding for member states.

Q14. Important areas of the countryside are maintained and kept open by which of the following organisations?

Answer: C – The National Trust

Q15. Which of the following statements is true?

Answer: A – At Christmas time, young children are taught that Father Christmas brings them presents on Christmas Eve

Q16. Alfred Hitchcock directed which of the following films:

Answer: D – The 39 Steps

Q17. The patron saint of England is St Charles. True or false?

Answer: B – False

Q18. Scotland was the only one of the home nations who failed to qualify for Euro 2016. True or false?

Answer: A – True

Q19. Why do some historians view the Iron Age as the beginning of recorded British history?

Answer: D – The people of the Iron Age created minted coins, inscribed with the names of kings.

Q20. The Statute of Rhuddlan attempted to establish English rule in Wales. True or false?

Answer: A – True

Q21. Why did the Glencoe Massacre take place?

Answer: A – The MacDonald clan of Glencoe were late for swearing fealty to William III.

Q22. In the UK, once you have voted, your vote will be published online for everyone to see. True or false?

Answer: B – False

Q23. Which two of the following are common features of the small claims procedure?

Answer: B – These cases are heard before a judge, without a jury, C – These cases are heard in a small room, without lawyers.

Q24. Which of the below statements is true?

Answer: A – Members of the School Board are responsible for making sure that the school adheres to and maintains high standards.

Test 3

Q1. Which two countries have their patron saint's day as a public holiday?

Answer: C – Northern Ireland, D – Scotland

Q2. David Hockney was a huge contributor to which 1960s movement?

Answer: B – The pop art movement

Q3. At the Battle of Waterloo, the British forces led by the Duke of Wellington, defeated the French forces led by:

Answer: B – Napoleon

Q4. Which of the following statements is true?

Answer: A – In 2007, Tony Blair was replaced as Prime Minister by Gordon Brown.

Q5. Which of the following is the most popular sport in the UK?

Answer: D – Football

Q6. Which two of the following criteria are covered by employment law?

Answer: A – Disputes over wages, D – Unfair dismissal

Q7. Every year, the Boat Race (a rowing event) takes place between which two of the following universities?

Answer: A – Oxford, D – Cambridge

Q8. The total value of the Crown Jewels amounts to an estimated minimum of:

Answer: B – 20 billion pounds

Q9. Henry VIII passed the Act of the Government of Wales. What was this?

Answer: B – An act that united England with Wales, and placed Welsh representatives in Parliament

Q10. What was the ultimate outcome of the English Civil War, for Charles I? *Answer: C – He was defeated and executed by beheading*

Q11. Who wrote the murder-mystery play, The Mousetrap?

Answer: C – Agatha Christie

Q12. Andy Murray is only the second male British tennis player to have won a Grand Slam, since 1936. True or false?

Answer: B – False

Q13. The UN was set up after which of the following global events?

Answer: B – WWII

Q14. Which of the below statements is true?

Answer: B – England no longer uses the death penalty. Instead, criminals are sent to prison.

Q15. Which of the below statements is true?

Answer: A – As an intelligence agency, GCHQ work to repel the threat from extremist organisations such as Islamic State.

Q16. Which two of the following are able to run for public office in the United Kingdom?

Answer: B – Teachers, D – Paramedics

Q17. The Council of Europe is responsible for which of the following:

Answer: A – For ensuring that the laws surrounding human rights are respected and adhered to in its member countries

Q18. Which of the following statements is true?

Answer: A – The satirical magazine Punch was published for the first time during the 1840s

Q19. Which two of the following were wives of Henry VIII?

Answer: C – Anne of Cleves, D – Catherine Parr

Q20. Along with Germany, which two countries actively participated in the annexation of areas of Czechoslovakia?

Answer: A – Poland and Hungary

Q21. Which of the following statements is true?

Answer: B – Howard Florey and Ernst Chain were the first scientists to work out how to use Penicillin as a medicine.

Q22. Which of the following statements is true?

Answer: B – Loch Ness is the second largest lake in Scotland

Q23. The White Tower, in the Tower of London, was built on the orders of which king?

Answer: B – William the Conqueror

Q24. The annual Remembrance Day Service is held at The Cenotaph. True or false?

Answer: A – True

Test 4

Q1. Which of the following statements is true?

Answer: B – One of the most important principles of The Enlightenment was that everyone should have the right to their own political and religious beliefs.

Q2. The Union Flag consists of how many crosses?

Answer: C – 3

Q3. Which of the below statements is true?

Answer: B – Taking the bus to work in the morning is a good way of creating less pollution.

Q4. The Loch Ness Monster has been scientifically proven to exist. True or false?

Answer: B – False

Q5. What is a constituency?

Answer: C – A small area of the country

Q6. The National Eisteddfod celebrates music, dance, art and other original performances. In which country is this held?

Answer: B – Wales

Q7. Which of the below statements is true?

Answer: B – UK Law states that you must be at least 16 years old to drive a moped, but 17 to drive a motorbike.

Q8. Which two of the following are NOT members of the Commonwealth?

Answer: B – Italy, C – Afghanistan

Q9. Under Queen Victoria, Britain repealed the Corn Laws. What was the result of this?

Answer: A – It became easier to import cheap raw materials – such as grain – which in turn bolstered British industry.

Q10. Which of the following statements is true?

Answer: B – Jane Seymour was Henry VIII's third wife. She was divorced.

Q11. From which time period does the poem *Beowulf* originate?

Answer: D – Anglo-Saxon

Q12. Sir Robin Knox-Johnston was the first person to accomplish which of the following:

Answer: B – Sailing single-handed around the world, without stopping

Q13. *The Golden Hand*, which belonged to Francis Drake, was one of the first ships to sail around the world. True or false?

Answer: B – False

Q14. Isambard Kingdom Brunel constructed which major transport means?

Answer: C – The Great Western Railway

Q15. Where in England will you find Anfield Stadium?

Answer: B – Liverpool

Q16. In the UK, Christians make up over half of the religious population. True or false?

Answer: A – True

Q17. Which of the following statements is true?

Answer: A – Ealing Studios has a claim to being the oldest continuously working film studio facility in the world.

Q18. What is the minimum age requirement to drive a car or motorcycle?

Answer: A – 17

Q19. Which of the following statements is true?

Answer: B – The British used fighter planes such as the Spitfire and the Hurricane to repel German forces.

Q20. Which of the following statements is true?

Answer: A – Julius Caesar was the first Roman leader to attempt an invasion of Britain.

Q21. The Grand National is a:

Answer: C – Horse race

Q22. In which country will you find the cities of Birmingham and Plymouth?

Answer: C – England

Q23. Snowdon is the highest point of which country?

Answer: A – Wales

Q24. Which of the following statements is true?

Answer: A – The Welsh language is completely separate to English.

Test 5

Q1. England are the only country in Great Britain with an international football cup win to their name. True or false?

Answer: A – True

Q2. Which of the following landmarks is built upon Castle Rock, part of an ancient volcano?

Answer: D – Edinburgh Castle

Q3. John Petts was an artist best known for his contributions to the field of abstract painting. True or false?

Answer: B – False

Q4. Which of the below statements is true?

Answer: A – Tax evasion in the UK is a serious offence.

Q5. Which of the below statements is true?

Answer: B – The UK police are a public service, who are unbiased and protect everyone.

Q6. Which two of the following were among the terms of the Treaty of Versailles?

Answer: A – Germany had to accept total responsibility for the war, C – Germany had to pay extensive reparation fees.

Q7. Which of the following statements is true?

Answer: B – Hadrian's Wall is a UNESCO World Heritage Site, and remains extremely popular with walkers.

Q8. What is 'panto'?

Answer: A – A type of musical comedy, performed on stage.

Q9. Like other TV channels, the BBC is funded through advertisements and subscriptions. True or false?

Answer: B – False

Q10. The European Convention on Human Rights was created by which of the following bodies?

Answer: C – The Council of Europe

Q11. William Shakespeare was born in Kingston upon Thames. True or false?

Answer: B – False

Q12. The role of the Speaker is to keep order during parliamentary debates. How is the Speaker chosen?

Answer: D – By the other MPs

Q13. The practice of female genital mutilation in the UK is illegal. However, it is legal to take a woman abroad to have this done. True or false?

Answer: B – False

Q14. Every single member of the Commonwealth belongs to the British Empire. True or false?

Answer: B – False

Q15. With which country is the meal Ulster Fry traditionally associated?

Answer: D – Northern Ireland

Q16. Towns and cities in the UK are governed by:

Answer: D – Local authorities

Q17. Which of the following statements is true?

Answer: A – Working together, Britain and France produced the first supersonic commercial airliner.

Q18. From 1853-1913, over 13 million people left Britain. True or false?

Answer: A – True

Q19. The Isle of Man is a:

Answer: C – Crown Dependency

Q20. Which of the following statements is true?

Answer: B – The Moderator of the General Assembly of the Church of Scotland is appointed for one year only.

Q21. Thomas Chippendale is famous for:

Answer: A – Designing furniture

Q22. The responsibilities of Police and Crime Commissioners include:

Answer: D – Setting the local policing budget

Q23. Which of the below statements is true?

Answer: B – Any man who forces a woman to have sex can be charged with rape, including the woman's husband.

Q24. In order to apply for a National Insurance Number, you will generally need to supply documents that prove your identity. True or false?

Answer: A – True

Test 6

Q1. The London Eye is situated in which position on the River Thames?

Answer: C – The south bank

Q2. The 'Divine Right of Kings' refers to the belief that the king has been chosen by God to rule. True or false?

Answer: A – True

Q3. What sparked the outbreak of World War I?

Answer: A – The assassination of Archduke Franz Ferdinand

Q4. In 1940, much to the shock of the world, Germany conquered which major European power?

Answer: C – France

Q5. Which food is traditionally eaten on Shrove Tuesday?

Answer: B – Pancakes

Q6. Which of the below statements is true?

Answer: A – In England and Wales, the small claims procedure is used for claims that amount to £5,000 or less.

Q7. Your National Insurance Number allows the government to track your National Insurance contributions. True or false?

Answer: A – True

Q8. Working people in the UK are required to pay income tax. What does this money go towards?

Answer: C – Roads, education and other public services

Q9. Diwali is celebrated by both Sikhs and Hindus. True or false?

Answer: A – True

Q10. People commemorate the 11th November by:

Answer: B – Wearing poppies and having a two minutes silence

Q11. The Prime Minister of the UK is a member of the House of Lords. True or false?

Answer: B – False

Q12. Which of the following statements is true?

Answer: A – Wilfred Owen was the writer of Anthem for Doomed Youth.

Q13. The Confederation of British Industry (CBI) are an example of a:

Answer: A – Pressure group

Q14. The longest distance on the UK mainland is between John O'Groats and Gillingham, Medway. True or false?

Answer: B – False

Q15. Which two of the following forms of disputes, can be settled under civil law?

Answer: A – Housing disputes, B – Workplace safety disputes

Q16. Which of the following statements is true?

Answer: B – The UK contains 15 national parks.

Q17. During the Middle Ages, what changes took place within the judging profession?

Answer: A – Judges began to be chosen by merit.

Q18. Which of the following statements is correct?

Answer: A – In the UK, Christmas is celebrated on the 25th December.

Q19. Which of the below statements is true?

Answer: B – People of the UK have total religious freedom and are free to believe in whatever they wish.

Q20. It is a legal requirement for BBC radio and television broadcasts to be politically balanced. True or false?

Answer: A – True

Q21. If you are a newly qualified driver in Northern Ireland, what type of plate must you display on your car?

Answer: C – An R plate

Q22. It is a legal requirement for each local authority to make its electoral register available for anyone to view?

Answer: A – True

Q23. What is the name for the period of political strife that occurred in Northern Ireland, beginning in the 1970s?

Answer: D – The Troubles

Q24. Proportional Representation is the name for the system by which MEPs are elected. True or false?

Answer: A – True

Test 7

Q1. When a defendant is found guilty in Crown Court, which of the following individuals decides upon the penalty?

Answer: C – The judge

Q2. In 55BC, Julius Caesar conquered Britain. True or false?

Answer: B – False

Q3. Which of the following statements is true?

Answer: B – In 1933, Adolf Hitler was named Chancellor of Germany.

Q4. Which two of the following forms of offence, can be charged under criminal law?

Answer: B – Carrying a weapon, D – Smoking in a public place

Q5. Which of the following statements is true?

Answer: A – The Domesday Book was introduced by William the Conqueror, after his invasion of 1066.

Q6. The Reform Act of 1832 increased the number of people who could vote. True or false?

Answer: A – True

Q7. Why was Hadrian's Wall constructed?

Answer: D – To keep out Scottish rebels, who were unhappy with the Roman invasion

Q8. Loch Ness is part of the Caledonian Canal. True or false?

Answer: A – True

Q9. Charlie Chaplin is famous for his part in which type of movies?

Answer: C – Silent movies

Q10. Scottish courts can deliver a verdict of 'not proven'. In this instance, what happens to the defendant?

Answer: A – They are released

Q11. Who opens the new parliamentary session each year?

Answer: C – The Monarch

Q12. Cowes is famous for hosting sailing events. Whereabouts is Cowes located?

Answer: D – The Isle of Wight

Q13. Which of the following statements is true?

Answer: A – You can participate in the National Lottery by buying a ticket from a shop.

Q14. *Auld Lang Syne* was written by which Scottish poet?

Answer: D – Robert Burns

Q15. Which of the following statements is true?

Answer: A – During the Bronze Age, people buried their dead in tombs called round barrows.

Q16. Coronation Street, Eastenders and Emmerdale are all examples of which type of TV programme:

Answer: C – Soap

Q17. If you owe a significant amount of money to someone, but are unable to pay, it is common practice for them to take you to court. True or false?

Answer: A – True

Q18. In the 2012 Olympics, Mo Farah won gold in the 6,000 and 12,000 metre races. True or false?

Answer: B – False

Q19. How did James I deal with Irish religious rebellions?

Answer: B – By encouraging Protestants to form 'plantations' in the northern province of Ulster

Q20. The penalty for watching TV without a licence can be up to:

Answer: A – A fine of £1,000

Q21. Which two of the following forms of income, will you need to pay tax on?

Answer: A – Employment wages, D – Pension money

Q22. Which of the following is a reason for Britain having tight border controls?

Answer: A – To prevent terrorists from entering the country

Q23. Which of the below statements is true?

Answer: B – The Same Sex Marriage Act of 2013 made it legal for people of the same sex to marry.

Q24. Which of the below statements is true?

Answer: A – Pay As You Earn is the name for the system where your income tax is automatically taken from your wages.

Test 8

Q1. In the UK, women receive the right to vote once they turn 21. Men can vote once they reach the age of 18. True or false?

Answer: B – False

Q2. Which of the below statements is true?

Answer: B – You won't be legally penalised for failing to recycle, but your bin men can refuse to take your rubbish.

Q3. If you are arrested by the police, then you will be taken directly to:

Answer: C – The police station

Q4. Which of the following statements is true?

Answer: A – In Northern Ireland, the anniversary of the Battle of the Boyne is a public holiday.

Q5. Which of the below statements is true?

Answer: B – In the UK, keeping your garden clean and tidy is a great way of demonstrating British values.

Q6. The UK government is formed by the party who wins the majority of:

Answer: A – Constituencies

Q7. A General Election is held every:

Answer: A – 5 years

Q8. Which of the following charities works to protect the environment?

Answer: B – Greenpeace

Q9. Which of the below statements is true?

Answer: B – In the UK, it is illegal to drink alcohol in public in some locations. You can be fined or arrested for breaking this law.

Q10. Which of the below statements is true?

Answer: B – If you own a car in the UK, you will be required to pay an annual vehicle tax.

Q11. On average, girls leave school with better qualifications than boys. True or false?

Answer: A – True

Q12. How many MPs are appointed by the Prime Minister, to act as cabinet ministers?

Answer: D – 20

Q13. Which of the following statements is true?

Answer: B – John O'Groats is located on the north coast of Scotland.

Q14. Florence Nightingale first came to prominence during the Crimean War. True or false?

Answer: A – True

Q15. Which of the following statements is true?

Answer: B – The first test of the British Atomic Bomb was named Operation Hurricane.

Q16. Where in Britain will you find Europe's longest dry ski slope?

Answer: D – Near Edinburgh

Q17. It is against UK Law to treat a pet with cruelty or neglect. True or false?

Answer: A – True

Q18. The United Kingdom consists of England, Scotland, Wales and the Republic of Ireland. True or false?

Answer: A – True

Q19. What is the Commonwealth?

Answer: C – A group of countries, who work together for the purposes of democracy and international development

Q20. Although Henry VIII created his own church, England remained Catholic until his death in 1547. True or false?

Answer: A – True

Q21. In 1066, the Battle of the Somme was fought between William of Normandy, and Harold Godwinson. True or false?

Answer: B – False

Q22. Sake Dean Mahomet introduced scissors as a tool to England. True or false?

Answer: B – False

Q23. The Industrial Revolution saw the development of which mass production process?

Answer: A – The Bessemer Process

Q24. The Gunpowder Plot was instigated by a group of disillusioned Protestants, who plotted to blow up the Houses of Parliament. True or false?

Answer: B – False

Test 9

Q1. Who printed *The Canterbury Tales*?

Answer: B – William Caxton

Q2. The Hundred Years War was fought between Britain and France. True or false?

Answer: A – True

Q3. On which bridge in London will you find a statue of a Boudicca, commemorating her efforts against the Romans?

Answer: A – Westminster Bridge

Q4. The Prime Minister of the UK can be forced to resign if the MPs in his party decide they need a change. True or false?

Answer: A – True

Q5. The distance from Land's End to John O'Groats is 870 miles. True or false?

Answer: A – True

Q6. London Fashion Week takes place three times a year.

Answer: B – False

Q7. Which of the following statements is true?

Answer: A – Roald Dahl was born in Wales.

Q8. Which of the following statements is true?

Answer: A – The Highland Clearances was the name for the demolishing of small farms, to make space for livestock.

Q9. Which of the following statements is true?

Answer: B – The Black Death of 1348 was the worst epidemic of disease ever to hit Britain.

Q10. During the Victorian Age, more than half of the world's iron, coal and cotton was produced by the UK. True or false?

Answer: A – True

Q11. NATO consists of which two of the following:

Answer: A – North American countries, C – European countries

Q12. Which of the following statements is true?

Answer: A – The Normans brought feudalism to England

Q13. Following the battle of Bosworth Field, Henry Tudor married which of the following women?

Answer: D – Elizabeth of York

Q14. Harold Pinter is a previous winner of the Nobel Prize in Literature. True or false?

Answer: A – True

Q15. Who was William Wilberforce?

Answer: B – An anti-slavery campaigner

Q16. During the War of the Roses, the sigil of House York was a white rose. True or false?

Answer: A – True

Q17. Feudalism is the name for a system where farmers united their farms into one collective farm. True or false?

Answer: B – False

Q18. On the 1st April, which event is celebrated up until 12 midday?

Answer: A – April Fools

Q19. The patron saint of England is St Charles. True or false?

Answer: B – False

Q20. Which of the following is an overseas British territory?

Answer: D – The Falklands Islands

Q21. In the UK, you must be 21 years or older to participate in gambling. True or false?

Answer: B – False

Q22. The artist Inigo Jones designed which of the following?

Answer: A – The Banqueting House in Whitehall, London

Q23. At present, there are more Jewish people than Hindu people in the UK. True or false?

Answer: B – False

Q24. V festival and the Isle of Wight festival are festivals of which kind?

Answer: B – Music

Test 10

Q1. Ian Fleming is the author of the well-known series, *Lord of the Rings*. True or false?

Answer: B – False

Q2. Sir Thomas Gainsborough was a famous British landscape painter. True or false?

Answer: B – False

Q3. Henry Moore is best known for:

Answer: C – His abstract sculptures

Q4. The expression 'bowled a googly' originates from which sport?

Answer: D – Cricket

Q5. If you are over the age of 75, then you are eligible to apply for a free TV licence. True or false?

Answer: A – True

Q6. Evelyn Waugh is best known for writing which of the following novels?

Answer: D – Brideshead Revisited

Q7. What type of church is the national Church of Scotland?

Answer: D – Presbyterian

Q8. Which sport does Dame Ellen MacArthur compete in?

Answer: A – Sailing

Q9. Colin Firth has never won an Oscar. True or false?

Answer: B – False

Q10. Which of the following statements is true?

Answer: B – Prior to Easter, Christians take a period of 40 days to reflect and prepare. This is known as Lent.

Q11. Which of the following statements is true?

Answer: B – On Remembrance Day, people wear poppies on their jackets, as a sign of respect for those who died in World War I.

Q12. The Ashes is a series of cricket matches played between England and which country?

Answer: C – Australia

Q13. What is the nickname for the huge bell outside of the Houses of Parliament?

Answer: C – Big Ben

Q14. The Crown Jewels are kept in Westminster Palace. True or false?

Answer: B – False

Q15. Alexander McQueen and Vivienne Westwood are leading brands in which industry?

Answer: D – The fashion industry

Q16. While most offenders between the ages of 10-17 will be tried in a Youth Court, serious cases can result in a different trial. True or false?

Answer: A – True

Q17. In Scotland, a verdict of 'not guilty' will see the defendant walk away freely. However, 'not proven' means that they must be re-tried. True or false?

Answer: B – False

Q18. In the UK, domestic violence is a crime which can be prosecuted. Domestic violence can be defined as:

Answer: C – When any person acts violently towards their partner

Q19. Which of the below statements is true?

Answer: B – Since 2012, England and Wales have had elected Police and Crime Commissioners.

Q20. Which of the below statements is true?

Answer: A – Britain played an essential role in the creation of the European Convention on Human Rights.

Q21. It is a legal requirement for you to register your car with which of the following:

Answer: C – The DVLA

Q22. What is canvassing?

Answer: B – When a member of a political party attempts to persuade others to support their candidate.

Q23. The modern Scottish parliament was formed in 1999. True or false?

Answer: A – True

Q24. Which of the following statements is true?

Answer: A – Chocolate eggs are given at Easter to celebrate the beginning of new life.

Test 11

Q1. Which of the following statements is true?

Answer: B – Eid al-Fitr is a Muslim festival, held to thank Allah for helping Muslims to complete their fast.

Q2. Which of the following statements is true?

Answer: A – During Diwali, there is a famous celebration that takes place in the city of Leicester.

Q3. Which of the following authors wrote both *Jude the Obscure* and *Far from the Madding Crowd*?

Answer: A – Thomas Hardy

Q4. If a game of Test Match cricket lasts for 5 days, the match is cancelled and the winner is the team that has the most runs. True or false?

Answer: B – False

Q5. Which of the following statements is true?

Answer: B – Mother's Day takes place three Sundays before Easter.

Q6. What is the Scottish equivalent of a County Court?

Answer: C – Court in Session

Q7. Even if you are suffering from a life-threatening illness, you are legally obligated to attend jury duty. True or false?

Answer: B – False

Q8. Which of the following statements is true?

Answer: B – Maiden Castle, which still exists today, is an example of an Iron Age hill fort.

Q9. Which of the following statements is true?

Answer: A – Admiral Nelson died in combat during the Battle of Trafalgar.

Q10. In 1851, the Great Exhibition opened in Hyde Park, Tottenham. True or false?

Answer: B – False

Q11. Which of the following has animator Nick Park won?

Answer: C – An Oscar

Q12. There is a National horseracing museum in Newmarket, Suffolk. True or false?

Answer: A – True

Q13. The London Eye contains 32 capsules, which can carry up to 25 people. True or false?

Answer: A – True

Q14. The UN has a Security Council, consisting of how many members?

Answer: D – 15

Q15. William Shakespeare wrote plays during the reign of:

Answer: D – Elizabeth I

Q16. Which of the following statements is true?

Answer: B – Richard III, of House York, was slain during the Battle of Bosworth Field in 1485.

Q17. Which of the following statements is true?

Answer: A – Henry VIII's son, Edward, was a devout Protestant.

Q18. Which of the following statements is true?

Answer: B – Following their successful invasion of Britain, the Romans tried and failed to conquer Scotland.

Q19. In the middle of the 19th century, Ireland suffered from which major disaster?

Answer: B – Famine

Q20. The Union Jack consists of three crosses. The cross of St George, the cross of St Andrew and the cross of:

Answer: C – St Patrick

Q21. Why were there tensions between the British government and their North American colonies?

Answer: A – The British government wanted to tax their North American colonies, who opposed this.

Q22. In 1721, Robert Walpole was named the very first British Prime Minister. True or false?

Answer: A – True

Q23. A 'rotten-borough' was the name for an area where the voting constituency was controlled by just one rich family. True or false?

Answer: B – False

Q24. Which of the following statements is true?

Answer: B – Following the defeat of the Vikings, many of the invaders remained in England, settling in an area known as Danelaw.

Test 12

Q1. Which of the following statements is true?

Answer: A – There is a statue of Boudicca on Westminster Bridge to commemorate her efforts in keeping the Romans at bay.

Q2. Which of the following statements is true?

Answer: B – The Fort of Vindolanda is a part of Hadrian's Wall.

Q3. D-Day is seen as significant, as it represented the beginning of the allies taking back key territories from Germany. True or false?

Answer: A – True

Q4. Who gave the speech, 'I have nothing to offer but blood, toil, tears and sweat'?

Answer: D – Winston Churchill

Q5. Which of the following statements is true?

Answer: A – Many of the best-known poets are buried in Poet's Corner at Westminster Abbey.

Q6. The 11th November 1918 is significant because this was the date that WWI ended. True or false?

Answer: A – True

Q7. In 1913, the British government implemented a bill that would allow for 'Home Rule' in Ireland. True or false?

Answer: B – False

Q8. Who did England fight against in the Boer War?

Answer: C – Netherlands

Q9. What was the Act of Union?

Answer: D – An act that created the Kingdom of Great Britain, and linked England and Scotland together.

Q10. How many children did Elizabeth I have?

Answer: D – 0

Q11. Which of the below statements is true?

Answer: B – If you are a non-UK National looking for work, and have permission to work in the country, you'll need to telephone the department for work and pensions, in order to obtain a National Insurance Number.

Q12. What does NSPCC stand for?

Answer: D – National Society for the Prevention of Cruelty to Children

Q13. Where is the UK national anthem most commonly played?

Answer: A – During important national occasions

Q14. Democracy is a system of government where all decisions are made by the Prime Minister and his cabinet. True or false?

Answer: B – False

Q15. What did the Chartists campaign for?

Answer: C – For every man to be allowed to vote

Q16. The National Citizen Service programme is responsible for organising the community service for young people who have committed crimes. True or false?

Answer: B – False

Q17. Which of the following is NOT a common responsibility of a Police Community Support Officer?

Answer: C – Delivering community service lessons to prisoners

Q18. Which of the following bodies investigates crime in the UK?

Answer: D – The police

Q19. Civil law does NOT cover debt issues. True or false?

Answer: B – False

Q20. Which of the below statements is true?

Answer: B – There are a number of refuges in the UK, designed to shelter sufferers of domestic abuse.

Q21. Which of the below statements is true?

Answer: B – The UK has a fairly low crime rate compared to the rest of the world.

Q22. Which of the following statements is true?

Answer: A – The British Pound is the oldest currency that is in use today.

Q23. Which of the following statements is true?

Answer: A – The Fenians advocated for complete Irish independence.

Q24. Which of the following statements is true?

Answer: A – The Battle of Agincourt was fought between Britain and France, during the Hundred Years War.

Test 13

Q1. Parliamentary proceedings are published in an official report, known as 'Hansard'. However, they are not shown on TV. True or false?

Answer: B – False

Q2. Which of the following statements is true?

Answer: A – George Frederick Handel was the composer of Music of the Royal Fireworks.

Q3. Which of the following statements is true?

Answer: A – The National Eisteddfod of Wales includes a number of competitions for Welsh poetry.

Q4. Which of the following statements is true?

Answer: B – Festival season in the UK takes place during the summer.

Q5. Which of the following people was instrumental in defeating the Spanish Armada in 1588?

Answer: C – Sir Francis Drake

Q6. Robert and George Stephenson were the father and son combination who pioneered which piece of technology?

Answer: B – The railway engine

Q7. The Battle of Hastings was fought between the forces of William of Normandy and Harold Hardrada. True or false?

Answer: B – False

Q8. Catherine of Aragon was Henry VIII's fifth wife. She was beheaded. True or false?

Answer: B – False

Q9. Why was 'Bloody Mary' nicknamed thusly?

Answer: C – She was nicknamed 'Bloody Mary' because of her harsh treatment towards Protestants.

Q10. One of the central themes of Rudyard Kipling's work was that the British Empire was a negative influence. True or false?

Answer: B – False

Q11. The Paralympics have their origin in the work of Sir John Senior, who worked at the Stoke Mandeville hospital. True or false?

Answer: B – False

Q12. Membership of the Commonwealth is entirely voluntary. True or false?

Answer: A – True

Q13. Ellie Simmonds was the youngest member of the British team at the 2008 Paralympic games. True or false?

Answer: A – True

Q14. Which of the below statements is true?

Answer: A – The European Convention on Human Rights provides British citizens with the right to free speech.

Q15. Which of the following annual events showcases garden design from Britain and around the world?

Answer: D – The Chelsea Flower Show

Q16. David Allan was a Scottish painter, who was best known for painting:

Answer: A – Portraits

Q17. The UK operates with a free press, meaning that newspapers and media in the UK are free from government control. True or false?

Answer: A – True

Q18. Wimbledon is the only Grand Slam tennis tournament that is played on:

Answer: A – Grass

Q19. Judges preside over disputes between organisations and members of the public. True or false?

Answer: A – True

Q20. What does PCSO stand for?

Answer: C – Police Community Support Officer

Q21. Arranged marriage in the UK is illegal. True or false?

Answer: B – False

Q22. The UK has no written constitution. This is because:

Answer: C – Britain has never had any revolution or uprising which required the government to create a constitution.

Q23. A judge is a professional who is responsible for interpreting the law, and ensuring that trials run in a smooth and fair fashion. True or false?

Answer: A – True

Q24. The Last Night of the Proms is held at which famous venue?

Answer: D – The Royal Albert Hall

Test 14

Q1. Which of the following statements is true?

Answer: A – Nearly 10% of the population has a parent or grandparent born outside of the UK.

Q2. Which two of the following are reasons for the rapid increase of the UK population in recent years?

Answer: B – Longer life expectancy, C – Increased migration

Q3. How are civil servants appointed?

Answer: B – Via an application process

Q4. James II was a fierce Protestant. True or false?

Answer: B – False

Q5. Which city is the capital of Scotland?

Answer: B – Edinburgh

Q6. The BAFTAs are the British equivalents of the Oscars. True or false?

Answer: A – True

Q7. Which of the following statements is true?

Answer: B – The main bank of the UK is known as the Bank of England.

Q8. Which of the following statements is true?

Answer: A – Northern Ireland contains people who speak Irish Gaelic, and people who speak English.

Q9. When did the term 'Scotland' first start to be used?

Answer: A – When the people of the North united under one king, to repel the Anglo-Saxons.

Q10. What is the Bayeux Tapestry?

Answer: C – A tapestry commemorating the events of the Battle of Hastings.

Q11. George I relied heavily on his ministers during his reign, as he suffered from a disability. True or false?

Answer: B – False

Q12. Richard Arkwright was a barber who went on to improve the way in which factory machines produced materials. True or false?

Answer: A – True

Q13. In 1918, the right to vote was given to women who were over the age of:

Answer: C – 30

Q14. At the end of the war, Hitler was arrested and put on trial for his war crimes. True or false?

Answer: B – False

Q15. The BAFTA awards are hosted by which of the following:

Answer: A – The British Academy of Film and Television Arts.

Q16. *Lawrence of Arabia* (1962) was directed by David Lean. True or false?

Answer: A – True

17. Which of the following statements is true?

Answer: B – The Council of Europe does not have the power to make laws.

Q18. Which of the following poets wrote, *Home Thoughts From Abroad*?

Answer: D – Robert Browning

Q19. Which of the following statements is true?

Answer: B – Following the mega-tsunami of 6100BC, southern marshlands were turned into the English Channel.

Q20. Which of the following statements is true?

Answer: B – The New Stone Age lasted from the first time that metal was used, until the first time that electricity was used.

Q21. Following his victory at the Battle of Hastings, William followed up by swiftly conquering Wales and Scotland. True or false?

Answer: B – False

Q22. Robert Bruce defeated the English at which battle?

Answer: C – The Battle of Bannockburn

Q23. Which of the following statements is true?

Answer: B – In 1922, Ireland split into two countries – Northern Ireland and the Irish Free State.

Q24. The first tennis club in England was founded in 1872, at which location?

Answer: D – Leamington Spa

Test 15

Q1. Which of the following statements is true?

Answer: A – The Swinging Sixties was nicknamed after the liberal development of fashion, music and cinema.

Q2. Which of the following statements is true?

Answer: B – From 1979 till 1990, Britain was run by a Conservative government.

Q3. The Wars of the Roses were fought between the supporters of which two families?

Answer: B – The House of York, D – The House of Lancaster

Q4. The Eden Project was opened in:

Answer: C – 2001

Q5. Wembley Stadium is located in West London. True or false?

Answer: B – False

Q6. If you wish to visit the House of Commons, or the House of Lords, you can queue up outside the building. True or false?

Answer: A – True

Q7. How many members of Scottish Parliament are there?

Answer: C – 129

Q8. Since 1999, hereditary peers have had the automatic right to attend the House of Lords. True or false?

Answer: B – False

Q9. The Chancellor of the Exchequer is responsible for which of the following:

Answer: C – UK economy

Q10. Which of the following statements is true?

Answer: B – FC Barcelona have played two Champions League finals at Wembley Stadium, and won both.

Q11. Henry Purcell was the organist at which famous Abbey?

Answer: A – Westminster Abbey

Q12. Britain, Wales and Northern Ireland compete together as one national football team. True or false?

Answer: B – False

Q13. In modern day 2016, there is now nothing left of Hadrian's Wall. True or false?

Answer: B – False

Q14. What is Constitutional Monarchy?

Answer: B – A system where the monarch cannot pass particular actions or laws, if parliament don't agree.

Q15. Queen Victoria was the longest serving monarch in British history. True or false?

Answer: B – False

Q16. From which war did the Victoria Cross originate?

Answer: D – The Crimean War

Q17. Which of the following statements is true?

Answer: A – In Scotland, minor criminal offences go to a Justice of the Peace Court.

Q18. Which of the below statements is true?

Answer: B – In England, you will be able to find the numbers of local solicitor services, in the Yellow Pages.

Q19. If you are self-employed, you don't need to pay National Insurance contributions. True or false?

Answer: B – False

Q20. People who are selected for jury duty are selected based on:

Answer: D – Random selection from people on the electoral register

Q21. A Youth Court can contain up to 3 special magistrates. True or false? *Answer: A – True*

Q22. if you are charged with murder in England, you will be tried in which of the following courts?

Answer: B – The High Court

Q23. Which of the below statements is true?

Answer: A – A solicitor is a type of lawyer, who will provide you with advice on legal issues.

Q24. Which of the below statements is true?

Answer: B – In Scotland, the system used to deal with young offenders is known as the Children's Hearing System.

Test 16

Q1. Which of the below statements is true?

Answer: B – England and Wales distinguish between the ages of offenders, and people of different ages will be subjected to different types of court/trial.

Q2. Which of the following statements is true?

Answer: A – In Northern Ireland, a system of youth conferencing is used to decide how child offenders should be dealt with.

Q3. The UK police have a duty to do which of the following:

Answer: A – To ensure that citizens of the UK feel safe, protected and free from disturbance to their daily lives.

Q4. In the UK, it is illegal to buy alcohol from a shop for anyone under the age of:

Answer: A – 18

Q5. Manchester and Cardiff are both capitals of countries in the UK. True or false?

Answer: B – False

Q6. The Eden Project, which houses plants from all over the world, is located in Cornwall, England. True or false?

Answer: A – True

Q7. The Proms lasts 8 weeks, and celebrates which of the following:

Answer: D – Orchestral music

Q8. Sir Arthur Conan Doyle was a pioneer in which genre of fiction?

Answer: B – Detective

Q9. In Scotland, the 2nd January is a public holiday. True or false?

Answer: B – False

Q10. In which year was the voting age changed from 21 to 18?

Answer: C – 1969

Q11. Women make up approximately what proportion of the UK workforce?

Answer: A – Half

Q12. Which of the following statements is true?

Answer: B – In the UK, more women than men study at university.

Q13. Which of the following statements is true?

Answer: A – In the UK, you will find women working in all sectors of the economy.

Q14. The Eden Project, in Cornwall, is home to which of the following:

Answer: D – Greenhouses and plants

Q15. The National Anthem of the UK starts with which of the following words:

Answer: D – God save our gracious Queen

Q16. MPs have a responsibility to do which TWO of the following:

Answer: A – To represent the people of their constituency in Parliament, D – To discuss critical national issues

Q17. In which theatre were Shakespeare's plays performed?

Answer: D – The Globe Theatre

Q18. Under Queen Victoria, Britain became the largest empire in history. True or false?

Answer: A – True

Q19. During the Crimean War, Britain was allied with which countries?

Answer: C – France and Turkey

Q20. Which of the following statements is true?

Answer: A – In 1833, the Emancipation Act completely abolished slavery of any kind in the British Empire.

Q21. Which of the following statements is true?

Answer: B – The First World War ended at 11am on the 11th November 1918

Q22. Britain became a member of the EU in 1973, but left in 2014. True or false?

Answer: A – True

Q23. Who of the following is a famous British film director?

Answer: A – Ridley Scott

Q24. In the UK, the role of a jury is to do which of the following:

Answer: A – Decide on whether the person is guilty or not guilty

Test 17

Q1. The Northern Ireland Assembly can be suspended at the behest of the UK Government. True or false?

Answer: A – True

Q2. In UK politics, what is the correct name for the second-largest party, at any given time?

Answer: D – The opposition

Q3. Complaints to the Police can only be made by writing directly to the Chief Constable of your local station. True or false?

Answer: B – False

Q4. In the UK, the police are independent of the government. True or false?

Answer: A – True

Q5. The Magna Carta of 1215, established which key principle?

Answer: C – That the king was subject to law, and had to consult with his noblemen to make key decisions

Q6. Which geographical event caused the creation of the English Channel?

Answer: B – A mega-tsunami

Q7. In 2012, the Queen celebrated which anniversary?

Answer: B – Her Diamond Jubilee (60 years as queen)

Q8. Which of the following statements is true?

Answer: B – Mary Queen of Scots was executed on the orders of her cousin, Queen Elizabeth I.

Q9. Which of the following statements is true?

Answer: A – The Peasant's Revolt of 1381 was a result of feudalism.

Q10. Which of the following statements is true?

Answer: A – The Great Fire of London started at a bakery on Pudding Lane.

Q11. Prime Minister's Questions, takes places how often?

Answer: B – Once every week

Q12. In Scotland, the small claims procedure is used to settle claims of under £5,000. True or false?

Answer: B – False

Q13. What is the title of the National Anthem of the UK?

Answer: C – God Save the Queen

Q14. It is a criminal offence to harass someone because of their ethnicity. True or false?

Answer: A – True

Q15. Youth Courts deal with individuals who are aged between 10 and 21 years old. True or false?

Answer: B – False

Q16. Every year, the Electoral Register is updated. This takes place during:

Answer: A – September or October

Q17. Which of the following statements is true?

Answer: B – Phil Taylor is the most successful darts player of all time.

Q18. Which of the following statements is true?

Answer: B – Mo Farah was born in Somalia. He is a long distance runner and Olympic champion.

Q19. Which of the following statements is true?

Answer: A – Video gaming is extremely popular in the UK.

Q20. What is a hill fort?

Answer: C – A well defended settlement, built on top of a hill

Q21. The Elizabethan Religious Settlement required any public or church officer member to swear allegiance to which monarch?

Answer: B – Elizabeth I

Q22. Which of the following statements is true?

Answer: A – Robert Burns was nicknamed 'The Bard'.

Q23. Historians are unanimously agreed that the Suffragettes helped the cause of women's votes. True or false?

Answer: B – False

Q24. Why did Huguenots come to Britain?

Answer: A – To escape from religious persecution in their own countries

Test 18

Q1. Towns and cities in the UK are governed by which of the following:

Answer: B – A democratically elected council, selected by the people living in the area

Q2. The House of Commons is formed by which of the following?

Answer: A – Elected MPs

Q3. Which of the following statements is true?

Answer: A – Approximately 21% of the British population identify themselves as atheist.

Q4. Which of the following statements is true?

Answer: B – The Monarch of the UK has the right to select the Archbishop of Canterbury.

Q5. Which of the following statements is true?

Answer: A – The Church of Scotland is governed by ministers and elders.

Q6. The Women's Franchise League aimed to give married women better employability rights. True or false?

Answer: B – False

Q7. Which of the following statements is true?

Answer: A – The Glorious Revolution was named thusly, because of the lack of bloodshed that it involved.

Q8. The mayor of a town acts as the leader of:

Answer: C – The local council

Q9. The UK has always had a democratic voting system. True or false?

Answer: B – False

Q10. If you are setting up as self-employed, you won't need a National Insurance Number. True or false?

Answer: B – False

Q11. Youth Court cases are often heard by a district judge. True or false?

Answer: A – True

Q12. You will not have to pay a fee to gain entrance to the public galleries in the House of Commons and the House of Lords. True or false?

Answer: A – True

Q13. The Queen plays a leading role in which of the following:

Answer: C – Acting as an ambassador for the UK

Q14. In the UK, women can be prosecuted for being violent towards their romantic partner. True or false?

Answer: A – True

Q15. Gaelic is still spoken in:

Answer: C – Scotland

Q16. Which of the following statements is true?

Answer: B – Stand-up comedy is a type of comedy where a comedian stands up and talks to a live audience.

Q17. Which of the following statements is true?

Answer: A – The BBC is the largest broadcaster in the entire world.

Q18. Which of the following statements is true?

Answer: A – Gilbert and Sullivan wrote comic operas, such as HMS Pinafore and The Mikado.

Q19. In which circumstance would a by-election take place?

Answer: A – In the event that the current MP of a constituency resigns/ is unable to continue with the role.

Q20. The House of Commons has the power to overrule the House of Lords. True or false?

Answer: A – True

Q21. The UK government has been forced to suspend the Northern Irish Parliament in the past. True or false?

Answer: A – True

Q22. Following WWII, who succeeded Winston Churchill as Prime Minister?

Answer: B – Clement Atlee

Q23. The 19th century Irish famine left many people with a feeling of resentment towards the British government. True or false?

Answer: A – True

Q24. Which of the following statements is true?

Answer: B – Hans Holbein was a painter in the 16th century. He was born abroad, but painted in Britain.

Test 19

Q1. England, Wales, Scotland and Northern Ireland all have their own established churches. True or false?

Answer: B – False

Q2. Which two of the following are denominations of British currency?

Answer: A – 10p, D – 20p

Q3. Which of the following statements is true?

Answer: A – Members of the public cannot attend youth courts

Q4. Which of the following statements is true?

Answer: B – It is illegal to sell tobacco products to anyone under the age of 18 in the UK.

Q5. Which of the following statements is true?

Answer: B – In the UK, it is illegal to cause offence to someone based on the colour of their skin, with no exceptions.

Q6. Voluntary work has little benefit to the community, and should be performed to benefit the individual undertaking the work. True or false?

Answer: B – False

Q7. The members of the House of Lords are known as 'peers'. True or false?

Answer: A – True

Q8. In which sport did Sir Bobby Moore compete?

Answer: D – Football

Q9. Both parents take equal responsibility for their children in a marriage. True or false?

Answer: A – True

Q10. There are usually two police constabularies for each area of the country. True or false?

Answer: B – False

Q11. Which of the following takes place three Sundays before Easter?

Answer: A – Mother's Day

Q12. In the UK, the government are able to interfere with the outcome of a trial. True or false?

Answer: B – False

Q13. Both Scotland and England use the same system to judge young people. True or false?

Answer: B – False

Q14. Who was Aneurin Bevan?

Answer: A – The Minister for Health under Clement Atlee

Q15. In the UK, the right to a fair trial is available to:

Answer: D – Everyone

Q16. Although it is illegal to distribute and sell drugs such as heroin and ecstasy, it is not illegal to buy them. True or false?

Answer: B – False

Q17. Julian Barnes, Ian McEwan and Hilary Mantel are all past winners of which prestigious prize?

Answer: B – The Man Booker Prize

Q18. Which of the following statements is true?

Answer: B – Religiously, Easter marks the day on which Jesus Christ rose from the dead.

Q19. Which of the following statements is true?

Answer: A – The day before Lent starts is known as Shrove Tuesday.

Q20. Which of the following statements is true?

Answer: B – Sir Gawain and the Green Knight tells the story of one of the knights at the court of King Arthur.

Q21. How much discount do blind people receive off the cost of their TV licence?

Answer: D – 50%

Q22. Sir Francis Chichester and his crew were the first people to sail around the world. True or false?

Answer: B – False

Q23. Which of the following statements is true?

Answer: B – Scotland and Northern Ireland use different forms of banknotes to England.

Q24. Which of the following statements is true?

Answer: A – In the UK, Christmas is traditionally celebrated by eating turkey.

Test 20

Q1. Which of the following statements is true?

Answer: B – Bank holidays in the UK have no religious significance.

Q2. Which of the following statements is true?

Answer: A – Frank Lauder directed The Belles of St Trinians (1954).

Q3. Which of the following statements is true?

Answer: A – The Turner Prize was named after Joseph Turner, an influential landscape artist.

Q4. The system in which MPs are elected is known as:

Answer: B – First past the post

Q5. The Prime Minister of the UK lives in 20 Downing Street. True or false?

Answer: B – False

Q6. Police officers in the UK are also tasked with participating in local schemes and initiatives, to benefit community wellbeing. True or false?

Answer: A – True

Q7. Which of the following sports originated in Scotland?

Answer: D – Golf

Q8. Which of the below statements is true?

Answer: A – If you are a non-UK national looking for work, then you will need a National Insurance Number.

Q9. Which of the below statements is true?

Answer: B – If you are working under the employment of someone else, your income tax will be paid directly to HMRC.

Q10. If you want to talk to an MP about a particular issue that concerns you, what should you do?

Answer: D – Attend a local surgery session

Q11. Volunteers are paid for the work that they do. True or false?

Answer: B – False

Q12. The House of Commons generally acts more independently from the government than the House of Lords. True or false?

Answer: B – False

Q13. The Scottish Parliament meets at Balmoral, to discuss key critical national issues. True or false?

Answer: B – False

Q14. Which of the below statements is true?

Answer: B – In the UK, when you die, it is optional for you to donate your organs to those who need them.

Q15. Which of the below statements is true?

Answer: B – You must be aged 18-70 to take part in jury duty.

Q16. Which of the below statements is true?

Answer: A – The British Red Cross is a charity, which aims to help people suffering from crisis.

Q17. If you suspect or know that someone is being forced into a marriage without consent, you can apply for protection orders on their behalf. True or false?

Answer: A – True

Q18. At Christmas, people traditionally give chocolate eggs as presents. True or false?

Answer: B – False

Q19. In England, you will need to bring photographic identification with you in order to vote. True or false?

Answer: B – False

Q20. If you feel that someone is trying to persuade you to join an extremist group, what should you do?

Answer: D – Contact the police

Q21. Which of the below statements is true?

Answer: B – Failing to pay enough National Insurance Contribution will result in you being unable to receive benefits such as a full retirement pension, or being unable to claim Jobseeker's Allowance.

Q22. Which of the below statements is true?

Answer: A – Court orders can be obtained to protect a person from being forced into a marriage, or to protect a person in a forced marriage.

Q23. It is illegal for the Monarch of the UK to give the Prime Minister political advice. True or false?

Answer: B – False

Q24. If you have a driving licence that has been obtained in France, you will be eligible to use this in the UK for a period of:

Answer: B – 12 months

Test 21

Q1. Police officers are not required to follow the laws that they uphold. True or false?

Answer: B – False

Q2. Which of the below statements is true?

Answer: A – It is a criminal offence to drive without motor insurance in the UK.

Q3. Which of the below statements is true?

Answer: B – Britain is one of the most liberal countries in the world, and frequently sets a good example to other nations.

Q4. Which of the below statements is true?

Answer: A – The UK is a high priority for terrorist organisations; as it is a rich, western country.

Q5. Which of these statements is true?

Answer: A – The term MEP stands for member of the European Parliament.

Q6. Civil law is used to settle disputes between which of the following:

Answer: A – Individuals and groups

Q7. If you wish to make a complaint about the police in Northern Ireland, then you can contact which of the following?

Answer: C – The Police Ombudsman

Q8. Which of the below statements is true?

Answer: A – If you are self-employed, then you will need to pay your own National Insurance Contributions, via a system called 'self-assessment'.

Q9. Which of the below statements is true?

Answer: B – In the UK, all young people are provided with a National Insurance Number just before their 16th birthday.

Q10. The members of the House of Commons are elected democratically. True or false?

Answer: A – True

Q11. Under Queen Victoria, Britain made changes to which of the following working laws?

Answer: C – Reducing the number of hours that women and children could work per day

Q12. In 1929, which negative event occurred, impacting countries all over the world?

Answer: B – The Great Depression

Q13. Which of the below statements is true?

Answer: A – If you are embroiled in a legal dispute, or have been charged with a crime, you can hire a solicitor.

Q14. Which of the below statements is true?

Answer: B – Hiring a solicitor in the UK can be expensive, and incur significant legal costs.

Q15. Florence Nightingale is seen by many people as the founder of modern nursing. True or false?

Answer: A – True

Q16. You must be of which minimum age in order to run for public office:

Answer: B – 18

Q17. Which two of the following countries compete in the Six Nations Rugby Championship?

Answer: C – Italy, D – France

Q18. Which of the following statements is true?

Answer: A – John Milton is the author of Paradise Lost.

Q19. Charles Stuart Parnell campaigned for Ireland to separate completely from the UK. True or false?

Answer: B – False

Q20. Which of the below statements is true?

Answer: A – If you have experienced domestic abuse, you can contact the Citizens Advice Bureau for guidance.

Q21. Who wrote the *Just So* stories?

Answer: D – Rudyard Kipling

Q22. Which of the below statements is true?

Answer: A – Individual police constabularies are headed by chief constables.

Q23. Which of the below statements is true?

Answer: A – At present, the biggest threat to the United Kingdom is from the so-called Islamic State, and other like-minded organisations.

Q24. Small claims are able to be issued online. True or false?

Answer: A – True

Life in the
UK Test

100s more practice
questions for free!

www.MyLifeInTheUKTest.net

NEED A LITTLE EXTRA HELP WITH BECOMING A BRITISH CITIZEN?

How2become have created two other FANTASTIC guides to help you prepare for the British citizenship tests.

These exciting guides are filled with essential tips and tricks, to ensure that your preparation is thorough, and that you are completely ready for the process ahead. With our help, you can secure your British citizenship today!

FOR MORE INFORMATION ON OUR GUIDES, PLEASE CHECK OUT THE FOLLOWING:

WWW.HOW2BECOME.COM